W. T. Wehrle · The Satiric Voice

Altertumswissenschaftliche
Texte und Studien

Band 23

William Thomas Wehrle
The Satiric Voice

1992
Olms-Weidmann
Hildesheim · Zürich · New York

William Thomas Wehrle

The Satiric Voice
Program, Form and Meaning in Persius and Juvenal

1992
Olms-Weidmann
Hildesheim · Zürich · New York

This work and all articles and pictures involved are
protected by copyright. Application outside the strict limits
of copyright law without consent having been obtained from
the publishing firm is inadmissable and punishable.
These regulations are meant especially for copies,
translations and micropublishings as well as for storing and
editing in electronic systems.

*

Das Werk ist urheberrechtlich geschützt.
Jede Verwertung außerhalb der engen Grenzen des
Urheberrechtsgesetzes ist ohne Zustimmung des Verlages
unzulässig und strafbar. Das gilt insbesondere für
Vervielfältigungen, Übersetzungen, Mikroverfilmungen
und die Einspeicherung und Verarbeitung
in elektronischen Systemen.

© Georg Olms AG, Hildesheim 1992
Alle Rechte vorbehalten
Printed in Germany
Umschlagentwurf: Prof. Paul König, Hildesheim
Herstellung: Druck Partner Rübelmann GmbH, 6944 Hemsbach
ISSN 0175-8411
ISBN 3-487-09613-7

FOR MARIE AND HANNIBAL: *FAMILIA QUIDEM OPTIMA*

To Anthony J. Boyle of the University of Southern California I express special gratitude for conscientiously given advice, emotive encouragement and honest friendship.

John P. Sullivan of the University of California, Santa Barbara, must likewise be thanked for his provision of sound editorial advice.

For any and all infelicities in *The Satiric Voice* the responsiblity of course rests with me alone.

CONTENTS

Introduction   1-4

Chapter 1: Program (and Meaning): Persius 1 and Juvenal 1 As Programmatic Satires

1. Persius' Prologue and Juvenal 1.1-14   5-12
2. Persius and Juvenal's Self-definition As Satirist; *Apologia Pro Opere Suo*   13-19
3. *Indignationis Materia*: The Satirists' Wrath Schematized   20-27
4. *Dissuasionis Reiectio*: The Satirists Commit Themselves   28-38

Chapter 2: Form (Persona/Voice): Personae In Persius and Juvenal

1. Persian Paradox: *Unus Ait Comitum*: Admixture of Voice   39-44
2. *Haec Crede Magistrum Dicere*: Socrates As Satirist   45-51
3. *Vatibus Hic Mos Est*: Anamnesis of *Satire* 1   52-56
4. Juvenal 15: *Homines Bestiis Inferiores*   57-62
5. Persona of Juvenal 3 (*Saturarum Auditor/Adiutor*: Umbricius)   63-70

Chapter 3: Form (Language): Persian and Juvenalian Language

1. Introduction: Vocabulary   71-80
1a. Greek Script in Juvenal   81
2. Juvenalian versus Persian Diminutive   82-85
3. Archaic Diction in Persius   86-88
3a. Archaic Diction in Juvenal   89-91
4. Imagery, Simile, Metaphor   92-97

Chapter 4: Form and Meaning: The Satirist's Message

1. The Philosophical Message in Persius   98-106
1a. The Philosophical Message in Juvenal   107-112
2. Society, Politics, Religion in Persius   113-115
2a. Society, Politics, Religion in Juvenal   116-126
3. Interrelationships of Form, Style and Meaning in Persius   127-133
3a. Interrelationships of Form, Style and Meaning in Juvenal   134-139

Bibliography   140-155

INTRODUCTION

Although the standard text for Juvenal and Persius remains the *OCT* of W. V. Clausen (1959),[1] more recent texts (both with commentaries) have been most helpful to me in parts of this work: e.g., J. Ferguson (1979) for Juvenal; G. Lee and W. Barr (1987) for Persius. Also the very early texts (and/or commentaries) of both Juvenal and Persius (e.g., those of Jahn/Bücheler [1851, 1893]; Mayor [1886]; Weidner [1889]; Conington [1893]; Friedländer [1895]; Duff [1898]) have proven to provide in places useful variant readings which are absent in much more recent editions. It will be noticed, therefore, that these early editions are frequently made reference to here, sometimes in pointed comparison/contrast to e.g., D. Bo (1969); R. Harvey (1981); E. Courtney (1980). Indeed, I have made use of all the texts and commentaries of Juvenal and Persius which have been available to me, and regret only that several early editions have been inaccessible for consultation. Nevertheless, merely for the sake of completeness, early as well as late texts are cited in my bibliography. Further, it will be noticed that this bibliography contains largely material which will not be cited in the body of the book. However, in choosing material for bibliographical inclusion, I have attempted to omit whatever would seem to have little direct bearing on issues touched upon herein, yet have tried to list all which might.

This work's title, *The Satiric Voice: Program, Form and Meaning* ..., only hints at the chapters' contents. I have attempted, whenever contingent, to comment on any aspect of Juvenal and Persius' satires which has appeared interesting (to me) or in need of (further) explanation. This study is not primarily comparative, although it does discuss Persius and Juvenal frequently in association. The central issues, therefore, toward which I have directed my discussion, are intertwined with exegeses on various questions incidental to these issues: formality of program; voice; language; ways in which form

---

[1] Forthcoming (February 1992) is a new edition of Juvenal and Persius (a revision of this earlier *OCT*) by W. V. Clausen.

(stylistic, poetic, etc.) relates to meaning, and how meaning (in some cases) predetermines form.

"If a text means everything, it means nothing."[2] Textual "meaning" is of utmost importance in the argument of this composition. Yet those meanings which I construct and/or suggest are, while often specific, generally, I hope, not overly restrictive in the eyes of the impartial observer. This book therefore necessarily conveys a literary methodology, yet in the conveyance of my own (idiosyncratic) perspectives on the complex, often elusive meanings imparted by the Persian and Juvenalian texts (and I begin with the assumption, contrary to certain [radical] theorists, that these texts do indeed imply an intrinsic nexus of meaning), I have made a conscious attempt not to remain enclosed within narrow methodological confines.

It is certainly the case that my reading of these texts is from a perspective not shared by all (or perhaps even, as a theorist might argue, by anyone, since no two readers can have exactly the same "response"). It has been my strict and consistent intention, however, to read with closeness--closeness intended to enhance my conception of the (literary) consciousness of the texts' original reader/writer. In a sense, I have remained a passive (although attentive) reader. This is to say that I have constructed meanings on the basis of what emerges from the "music" of the texts themselves rather than on the basis of an active application of predetermined critical guidelines (theory). In short, my method involves the following: a study of the text with consistent consideration of literary-historical context; attention to the possible influences of authors (especially satiric) prior to Persius and Juvenal and these satirists' responses to previous authors; a critical

---

[2] Boyle (1986) 2. For a concise and refreshing overview of the textual "reinterpretations" of such theorists as J. Derrida, E. Hirsch and R. Barthes (as applied to the classical text), see Boyle 1-14 especially ("Introduction: The Failed Text"). Although Boyle's discussion focuses primarily on Vergil's compositions, his comments are more generally applicable (just as theoretical ideologies are frequently thrown, like blankets, over whatever their adherents seek to cover).

assessment of (declared and implied) programmatic intentions; an attempt to appreciate developments in persona (voice); a consideration of how form and meaning co-depend, co-determine, or simply interrrelate: socio-ethical commentary versus poetic (aesthetic) formality.

My avoidance of (popular) theoretical approaches is deliberate, and I offer only a single apology. My (slight) comprehension of such approaches has produced not a growing enthusiasm, but only a kind of sceptical (even cynical) despondency; one directs himself away from the text only to traverse a quagmire of vague generalizations, none of which seems to provide a firm stepping stone. Yet, fearing lest we overlook or underestimate the significance of our exertion, we step tentatively from one stone to the next, all the while trying to convince ourselves that we know the nature of our progress. And, once we feel we have reached the terminus of this intellectual (theoretical) quagmire, still with hopes of finding at the other side novel levels of perception, we realize, if we are honest with ourselves, that we have crossed over only to a level of insignificance which is probably not novel, hardly even perceptible. The futility of our excursion is finally confirmed, meaninglessness becomes for us a reality to be avoided, and all that remains is a desire to return whence we started (if we can remember where that was). The necessity of the text to describe and perhaps explain itself is again acknowledged, we try to shake the muddy remnants of the theoretical quagmire from our intellectual shoes, and once again we allow ourselves to read the text. Closely.

To those who might assert that a disclaimer of theoretical doctrine itself indicates (or amounts to) established theory, I must admit the validity of their view. I will admit too that parallels might be drawn between my approach and those of earlier (classical) scholars. Yet I do not believe that this work suffers from deficiencies which can be remedied by the imposition of (currently popular) theoretical approaches--approaches which I am able neither to employ astutely (perhaps) nor embrace enthusiastically (certainly).

The strengths of this work derive not from the ingenious application of one or more general (theoretical) concepts, but rather from engagement to detail. Those therefore who seek in this book's pages an overall unity of argument based on an easily identifiable conceptual framework will fail. Those inclined to eschew the abstract in favor of the precise will, it is hoped, succeed in finding here inferences of which (textual) detail is an essential component.

CHAPTER 1

PERSIUS 1 AND JUVENAL 1 AS PROGRAMMATIC SATIRES

1. Persius' *Prologue* and Juvenal 1.1-14

In this section I will present an examination of the professed and implied purposes of Persius and Juvenal. (Necessarily, their attitudes toward the satiric traditions established by Lucilius and Horace must be given some consideration, but these will not be strongly stressed here). Simultaneously, we will consider the reasons given by Persius and Juvenal (hereafter to be referred to as P. and J. respectively) for choosing to compose satire rather than to follow another literary genre (*apologia pro opere suo*). This discussion will take the form of a step-by-step systematic analysis; comparative aspects of P.1 and J.1 are therefore presented *passim* as is appropriate.

Evidence derived from the manuscript tradition of the Persian corpus has led most students now to believe that the fourteen choliambic lines in which P. denies divine poetic inspiration were intended originally to precede *Satire* 1; thus taken, they form a prologue.[1] In this prologue the poet's primary emphasis is of course on the subject of traditional (e.g., Hesiodic) poetic inspiration.[2] The denial of such inspiration is, on the part of P., outright:

> Nec fonte labra prolui caballino
> nec in bicipiti somniasse Parnaso
> memini, ut repente sic poeta prodirem. (*Prol.* 1-3)

and:

> ... ipse semipaganus

---

[1] For discussion on the placement of the choliambs see e.g., Clausen (1956) preface.

[2] P.'s pointed rejection and criticism re. the "dream on Helicon" as divine intervention by Muses for poets is directed not only at the Hesiodic tradition, but also at that custom which was subsequently maintained by e.g., Callimachus (*Aet.* 1), Ennius (*Ann.* 1. 2-5), Propertius 3.3. By renouncing Helicon, P. at once defines his own (poetic) status and initiates an aggressive incursion against those of his contemporaries who might pretend to some degree of traditional (divine) poetic inspiration.

ad sacra vatum carmen adfero nostrum. (*Prol.* 6-7)[3]

The opening language of the prologue immediately strikes the reader as paradoxical. It is at once personal (e.g., the 1st person references in *prolui, memini, prodirem*), colloquial (*fonte ... caballino*, a markedly jocose and likewise contemptuous phrase for illustrious Hippocrene), yet poetical (e.g., the alliterative phrases *somniasse Parnaso; repente ... poeta prodirem*) and originally experimental (*ipse semipaganus ... carmen adfero*).[4]

Interpretations of *semipaganus*, 6, vary. The word is found nowhere else in Latin literature and is thus recognized as a unique Persian coinage.[5] What P. means by calling himself a "half-member of the *pagus*"[6] *may* be that P. does not consider himself qualified "to be in the company of *vates,*"[7] yet this interpretation works only on a superficial level. We will do better to interpret the *semipaganus* reference as indicative of the larger satiric program of P., a program wherein classes of poets are deliberately distinguished and sharply contrasted. (*Vates*, P.'s poetic contemporaries, will in fact be satirized *passim*, yet consistently in the satires). It is a mistake to think that P. is being modest or "self-

---

[3] *Carmen* is not merely, "a dignified term for P.'s satire" Harvey (1981) 12, but is ironic, pointing up the deliberate disparity between P.'s "song" and those of the "higher" genres (e.g. Epic).

[4] Of note also is P.'s choice of scazons ("limping iambics") for the prologue. Harvey (1981) 9 notices two aspects: "... a metre was required which set the Prologue apart from the other poems and which had at least some association with satirical themes (cf. Hipponax, Catullus)." But there is another possible aspect, significant programmatically. P.'s subject here is poor poesy; a "limping" meter is therefore appropriate in describing poets who are themselves "limp" in respect to style, production, even inspiration.

[5] Translations implying "half-rustic" (as suggested by the scholia), half-poet, half-learned, etc. are probably misleading. If *semipaganus* was indeed coined here by P. (as is evidently the case), its appearance would certainly have forced the *Prologue*'s original readership to assess its meaning. While the prefix *semi-* suggests 'half-,' a translation 'half-countryman,' the most apparent connotation of the word, fails to allow for the plurality of meaning which *semipaganus* would have originally embraced. *Pagus*, for example, from which *paganus* is derived, is related to the verb *pangere*. Apart from meanings of 'set, arrange, plant,' etc. in a general sense, *pangere* meant 'to compose poetry' (Cf. e.g. Cic. *Fam.* 16.18.3: *an pangis aliquid Sophocleum?*; Lucr. 1.25: *versibus ... quos ego de rerum natura pangere conor*). Thus the sense of *semipaganus* as 'half-composer' emerges, a sense more attuned to Persius' mock poetic disclaimer than that of 'half-countryman/rustic,' etc.

[6] Harvey (1981) 11.
[7] Ibid.

deprecatory"[8] here. In fact, far from considering himself either unqualified or unworthy of writing poetry, P. is deliberately divorcing himself from the traditional class of poets. His satire is separate and distinct from the poetic corpus of the bards whom he mentions (*ad sacra vatum carmen adfero nostrum*, 7). What P. means by calling himself a *semipaganus* is that he is not, and would not wish to be, a *vates* at all. We may even suggest that *vates* is for P. a term of abuse--a term which denotes pretension, whereas *poeta* does not carry such a derogatory connotation. (We will see that mere hope of money cannot create a *poeta* in P.'s view, yet *vates* evidently abound. Perhaps, therefore, one of the important distinctions P. is making in the prologue is between *vates* and [himself as] *poeta*).

The poetic style of the prologue is itself an index of the larger satiric program. P.'s much discussed *iunctura acris* (e.g., *cantare ... Pegaseium nectar, Prol*. 14) is neither unfortunate accident of linguistic indecorum nor symptom of ill-conceived poetic style.[9] Rather, it is indicator and amplifier of the satirist's *indignatio*. P. *deliberately* and with express purpose (i.e., to accent the unoriginality of more "traditional" poets) inserts these (apparently) discontinuous *iuncturae acres* into contexts which intend to upset and even break down formal poetic ('vatic/bardic') convention. P.'s is an attack on style-- style of course reflects men and *mores*; thus his disintegration of poetic style suggests his

---

[8] *OLD* sub *semipaganus*: "Word applied by Persius to himself in a self-deprecatory sense, as an unworthy member of the 'religious guild' of poetry."

[9] The employment of "sharp juxtapositions" by P. is discussed especially by Dessen (1968). Innumerable critics have been perplexed by P.'s "unorthodox" and "obscure" use of language; this of course justifies their conclusion that P. was himself a poor and unoriginal (see the irony) poet. (As recently as 1982, for example, N. Rudd [1982] 507 remarks on the weakness and irrelevance of P.'s fourth satire: "The satire as a whole ... is rather weak. The ridicule of the demagogue Alcibiades has little bearing on imperial Rome. The sequence of thought is sometimes confusing." Cf. also Rudd 510 on P.'s poetry in general: "These limitations [Stoic interest, intolerance, limited perspective, etc.] disqualify Persius from greatness ...". P. Connor (1988) 55 fortunately, however, perceives P.'s *iunctura acris*, for example, as imparting to his verse "a sharp ferocity of expression and a certain aggressively extravagant imagination." Indeed, essential to P.'s programmatic divorce of himself from typical *vates* is his unique (individual) and virulently original phraseology.

ultimate purpose--to dissolve the value-assumptions of a society bonded by corruption, perversion, immorality.

Equally complementary to the preliminary Persian satiric program as presented in this prologue is the attack on the creative resources of other (contemporary) poets; while their passion for poetic production may be sincere (real), it is nevertheless base, amounting only to the most primitive excitant: hunger. Even birds are motivated by it, and their motivation (like that of the poets whom P. attacks) gives rise to nothing original, but to mere repetition, duplication of what they have heard before:

> quis expedivit psittaco suum 'chaere'
> picamque docuit verba nostra conari?
> magister artis ingenique largitor
> venter, negatas artifex sequi voces. (*Prol.*8-11)

And it is the prospect of indulgence which motivates these mercenary poets; *venter,* 11, is a boldly stark term which can refer not only to the parrot and magpie, but transferred to the larger context of (Neronian) literary society, the term might conjure up images of sloth, sluggishness, *appetentia, luxuria.*[10]

Another reference to the bloated *venter* is made by P. in *Satire* 3, where an over-stuffed gourmand, despite his friend's advice against bathing on an over-filled stomach, takes himself to the bath, the result being a grotesque death:

> turgidus hic epulis atque albo ventre lavatur,
> gutture sulpureas lente exhalante mefites.
> sed tremor inter vina subit calidumque trientem
> excutit e manibus, dentes crepuere retecti,
> uncta cadunt laxis tunc pulmentaria labris. (3.98-102)

---

[10] J., perhaps in deliberate recollection of P., uses *venter* in *Satire* 4 to describe metonymically one of the perverse advisors present at the emperor's council regarding the *spatium admirabile rhombi* (4.39):
   Montani quoque venter adest abdomine tardus (4.107).
Here Montanus actually *is* a belly, made slow by its apparently insatiable and gluttonous *abdomen.*

The key word in 98 is *turgidus*, and this is amplified by *albo ventre*. Bellies are for P. indicators of the inflated, and especially the over-inflated or perversely inflated.[11] The gourmand in the above passage has become *turgidus* by perverse over-indulgence, the motivator of which is of course the *venter*, itself become pale and stretched beyond normal limits. Likewise, poets whose *ventres* are the literal and figurative motivators of "genius" (*magister artis ingenique largitor, Prol.* 10), overcome by the impulses of greed, lust and hunger, attempt poetic creation which is quite beyond their nature: (*negatas voces, Prol.* 11, is entirely appropriate not only to birds, but also to mercenary and unoriginal poets). Similarly, what is produced by such poets is, like the satiric belly, *turgidus*[12]

One of the most salient aspects of P.'s prologue is its almost immediate incursion into what we might aptly call poetic excess--an excess which manifests itself, according to both P. and J., in (mercenary) poetry which, while aiming at grandeur, achieves only immense dilation. And complementary to this point is P.'s implied assertion that truly (well)-inspired poetry is not born of mercenary intent:

> quod si dolosi spes refulserit nummi,
> corvos poetas et poetridas picas
> cantare credas Pegaseium nectar? (*Prol.* 12-14)[13]

---

[11] One cannot help but recall here the Muses of Hesiod, who describe mortal men as "mere bellies" at *Theog.* 26: ποιμένες ἄγραυλοι, κάκ᾽ ἐλέγχεα, γαστέρες οἶον. Thematically, P.'s poets, motivated by appetite alone, parallel the "gastric" shepherds of Hesiod.

[12] Cf. J. 1.4-6: *ingens/Telephus aut summi plena iam margine libri/scriptus et in tergo necdum finitus Orestes?*). And it is remarkable also that J. too includes in his program the motif of the bloated gourmand who meets his end in the bath:
> poena tamen praesens, cum tu deponis amictus
> turgidus et crudum pavonem in balnea portas.
> hinc subitae mortes atque intestata senectus. (1.142-44)

[13] In punctuating the end of v. 14 with a question mark, I follow the plausible suggestion of Harvey (1981) 9. Despite most edd. preference for the full stop here, the question mark seems to yield the better sense, since the "belief" implied is both incredible and absurd.

The implication here again depends upon our understanding of the ravenous *venter*; mere greed and bestial appetite (stressed appropriately by analogies to the parrot, magpies and crows) can in no way inspire the innately untalented. Otherwise, implies P., we would have to believe that crows and magpies, if sufficiently rewarded, were capable of composing poetry worthy of the gods' ears (*Pegaseium nectar*).

J. of course does not grace his *Satires* with a prologue of any kind. But his attack upon the distended yet inane poetry of his day is no less immediate than that of P. Indeed the first fourteen lines of *Satire* 1 seem to correspond programmatically to P.'s prologue. J. inverts somewhat the Persian program, however. He does not begin immediately, as does P., with a mock *apologia*. Rather, he introduces himself and his subject with the brief, although anticipatory, question, *Semper ego auditor tantum?* (1.1). The personal nature of the Juvenalian satiric program is realized at once (*ego*); the satirist's impatience and intolerance are hinted at (*semper* ... which is then contrasted with its opposite, *numquamne*, 1.1.); and then we are drawn directly into the specific roots of the satirist's *indignatio*: he has been a listener only (*auditor tantum*) and has an obsessive desire to repay torturously bad poets:

```
              ... numquamne reponam
vexatus totiens rauci Theseide Cordi?
inpune ergo mihi recitaverit ille togatas,
hic elegos? impune diem consumpserit ingens
Telephus aut summi plena iam margine libri
scriptus et in tergo necdum finitus Orestes? (1.1-6)
```

Satire 1.1-6 contains pregnant language which is no less impressive than that of P.'s prologue. Various compositional tactics combine here to draw the reader forcefully into the Juvenalian program. First are the sharp rhetorical questions, four in all, and the language itself is remarkably forceful: *reponam* (1); *vexatus* (2); *impune*, strengthened by its repetition (3,4). The contempt of the satirist for his vexatious reciters is confirmed mechanically: e.g., the harsh-sounding *rauci* ... *Cordi* (2), in which case the hoarseness of the satirized is countered with that of the satirist in his description; cf. also the over-extended description of an equally over-extended *Orestes* (6): *summi plena iam margine libri/scriptus et in tergo necdum finitus* (5-6).

And, like P.'s iterative birds, J.'s bad poets merely repeat wearily exhausted themes; stale material is imparted dryly by the uninspired:

> nota magis nulli domus est sua quam mihi lucus
> Martis et Aeoliis vicinum rupibus antrum
> Vulcani; quid agunt venti, quas torqueat umbras
> Aeacus, unde alius furtivae devehat aurum
> pelliculae, quantas iaculetur Monychus ornos,
> Frontonis platani convolsaque marmora clamant
> semper et adsiduo ruptae lectore columnae. (1.7-13)

Thus J. is all too familiar with the stock poetic themes of contemporary poets; he knows them better, in fact, than anyone knows his own house, and he wants no part of them. And this is naturally J.'s way of divorcing himself from his fellow *litterati*. He too could treat these themes but, like P., he will set himself apart (cf. P.'s *Prol.*: *Heliconidasque pallidamque Pirenen/illis remitto quorum imagines lambunt/hederae sequaces*,4-6).

Stock (mythological) themes are disparaged, with the resulting implication that *anyone* could treat them: e.g., the terse expressions *quid agunt venti* (11); *alius* (10) in reference to the mythological hero Jason, and the famous Golden Fleece referred to merely as *furtivae ... aurum/pelliculae* (10-11). And, just as P.'s bird-poets might aspire to create divine poetry if bribed, so too do J.'s least gifted:

> expectes eadem a summo minimoque poeta. (1.14)

And the impression formed deliberately here by J. is quite on a par with that of P: literary taste has declined; contemporary poets have formed a homogeneous body wherein nothing outstanding can be detected.[14] Where P.'s prologue differs most notably from J.

---

[14] Horace likewise presents (like P. and J.) a standard *recusatio* on epic themes. Cf. e.g., *Serm.* 2.1.10-15, where Horace's interlocutor, who advocates epic, is answered sarcastically:
> 'aut si tantus amor scribendi te rapit, aude
> Caesaris invicti res dicere, multa laborum
> praemia laturus.' cupidum, pater optime, vires

1.1-14, however, is in the prologue's emphasis on money, bribery, greed and appetite. J.'s primary complaint is not that bad poets are necessarily greedy or mercenary, but rather that they have managed to gain status as legitimate bards, with the result that they ceaselessly burden their listener with trite and annoying recitations. Furthermore, the subject matter treated by these bards is irrelevant, with the result that the lecture parks are now not places of enjoyment and relaxation, but rather centers of unending torture:

> Frontonis platani convolsaque marmora clamant
> semper et adsiduo ruptae lectore columnae. (1.12-13)

The imagery here is of course humorous, but nevertheless grotesque; even insensate marble cannot bear the interminable *lector*. And thus again we are reminded of P.'s imagery of unnatural swelling; the implied turgidity of his monstrous *venter* relates to a poetic style as well as to a society whose salient characteristic is the unnatural inflation of deformity, perversion. While J. does not adapt directly for the context of the recital and *lector* P.'s imagery of swelling, his image of fracture (*ruptae*) approximates and functions in a way which is similar to that of P.'s *venter*. J.'s bad poets protrude; their multiplication has manifested itself in a collective body which is not only overgrown, but which has also become unavoidable, and can break stone simply by its oppressive voluminosity, durability, persitent prolixity.

Thus after pointing out the faults of their respective literary worlds, both P. and J. have set themselves apart from them. And yet since each is himself a poet, he must write; each will write therefore in the only appropriate "genre" left open to an original poet: *satura*. And after declaring that he will write satire, each poet enumerates the things he will censure.

> deficiunt: neque enim quivis horrentia pilis
> agmina nec fracta pereuntis cuspide Gallos
> aut labentis equo describat vulnera Parthi.

It is precisely *multa laborum/praemia* to which P. and J. both object also. Horace's *vires/deficiunt* is a clever and ironic way of saying that (historical) epic is not where his poetic impulses can be realized.

2. Persius and Juvenal's Self-definition As Satirist; *Apologia Pro Opere Suo*

Let us examine first how P., and then J., declare themselves satirists. P.'s introduction to the satiric format is, like that of J., Lucilian. But P.'s Lucilian prelude is elliptical and sudden; *Satire* 1 begins, in fact, with an actual quote from the "father of satire" (if we take the scholiast as correct here):

O curas hominum! o quantum est in rebus inane! (1.1)[15]

Thus P.'s reader is at once alerted that the subject to be treated involves "the cares of mankind" and the inanity of human affairs-- the traditional *lanx satura* of satire. J., in contrast, makes a less directly Lucilian appeal; he first promotes himself as equally qualified as other contemporary writers:

et nos ergo manum ferulae subduximus, et nos
consilium dedimus Sullae, privatus ut altum
dormiret. (1.15-17)

And since so many papyri are destined to be wasted by poor writers anyway, J. will not forfeit his opportunity:

... stulta est clementia, cum tot ubique
vatibus occurras, periturae parcere chartae.[16] (1.17-18)

Thus the natural introduction to his satiric theme; and his polite request for an audience is combined with the programmatic Lucilian appeal:

---

[15] The resemblance between this (Lucilian) verse and Lucretius 1.330, 569, and 2.14 has been observed (e.g., by Harvey [1981] 13-14). It is of course possible that Lucretius influenced P. here, but equally possible that Lucilius influenced Lucretius. As Harvey notes, "an allusion to the inventor of satire is, at this point in the poem, infinitely more appropriate than an echo of Lucretius." Contrast Zetzel (1977) 40-41: "... reference to Lucretius makes perfectly good sense here." Although Zetzel argues in detail for Lucretian influence (taking into account previous arguments, including that of Henss [1954] 159-61), his assertion that the notion of Lucilian influence stemmed from a mis-guided scholiast fails to convince; Zetzel himself (42) admits finally: "We will never know for certain whether Persius was alluding to Lucilius or Lucretius in his opening verse."

[16] J.'s use of *vatibus* here reminds us of the *vates* of P.'s prologue. The term is sarcastic, again (just as in P.) implying pretension and drawing a distinction between contemporary *vates* ("bards") and the satirist, who would evidently not wish to be counted among them.

> cur tamen hoc potius libeat decurrere campo,
> per quem magnus equos Auruncae flexit alumnus,
> si vacat ac placidi rationem admittitis, edam.[17] (1.19-21)

The language of the above passage introduces images of spectacle (*decurrere campo*, 19) and competition (*equos ... flexit*, 20). J. thereby recalls Lucilius' justly renowned boldness, courage, aggressiveness (J. implies therefore that he too will risk, by writing satire, censorship, exile, etc. But, as will be seen, J. makes provisions against this).

At *Satire* 1.2 P. promptly embarks upon an *apologia pro opere suo*. An imaginary interlocutor is introduced immediately to occasion P.'s defence of his undertaking (this anonymous adversary's fictive nature is confirmed at 1.44: *quisquis es, o modo quem ex adverso dicere feci*):

> "quis leget haec?" min tu istud ais? nemo hercule. "nemo?"
> vel duo vel nemo. "turpe et miserabile." quare?
> ne mihi Polydamas et Troiades Labeonem
> praetulerint? nugae. non, si quid turbida Roma
> elevet, accedas examenve inprobum in illa
> castiges trutina nec te quaesiveris extra. (1.2-7)

P.'s declaration is quite simple and straightforward here. The satirist admits that his work will be unpopular, his readers none or maybe two. But the primary point is that the literary preferences of Rome provide an unreliable criterion for the judgement of literature in general. One (P.) should write not for the taste of the unbalanced Roman audience, as does Labeo, the translator of well-known epic, but rather produce what stems from internal inspiration. Likewise, P. urges an audience (reader) to evaluate literature from a personal perspective (*nec te quaesiveris extra*, 7) rather than from the perspective of a *turbida Roma* which has proven itself a poor literary judge. Thus there is an implied

---

[17] Ferguson (1979) 113 re. v. 21: "The courteous tone lulls us;". Yet the invitation on J.'s part is not so much "courteous" as admonitory. *Si ... rationem admittitis* counsels the reader; the force is more to the effect of, "If you are willing patiently to open your minds to reason and to accept that my reasons (for writing satire) are valid ..."

antithesis: P. on the one hand, and the bird-poets of the prologue (exemplified here especially by Labeo) on the other.

J. integrates his *apologia* within specific exempla of vice as *Satire* 1 progresses. The poem is scattered, like the subjects it treats. Absurdities are intoduced at 1.22 and specified consecutively until the climactic declaration of 1.30: it would be more difficult *not* to write satire. J. reveals no preoccupation with the prospect of an audience, as does P. In contrast, J. lets his subjects call attention to themselves; the self-reflectiveness of the Persian program is suppressed. Yet the personal nature of J.'s *indignatio* is manifest:

> cum tener uxorem ducat spado, Mevia Tuscum
> figat aprum et nuda teneat venabula mamma,
> patricios omnis opibus cum provocet unus
> quo tondente gravis iuveni mihi barba sonabat,
> cum pars Niliacae plebis, cum verna Canopi
> Crispinus Tyrias umero revocante lacernas
> ventilet aestivum digitis sudantibus aurum
> nec suffere queat maioris pondera gemmae,
> difficile est saturam non scribere. (1.22-30)

There is here, therefore, a brief inversion of the Persian program. The absurd practices which the satirist has observed *lead up to* his first *apologia*, whereas P. supplies a more gradual justification for writing satire, and then follows it with an attack on, again, perverse poetasters.

P.'s first *apologia* culminates at 1.12: *sed sum petulanti splene--cachinno*.[18] Thus P. *must* satirize; his innate character is insolent, and its release manifests itself in impudent themes. And what exactly is it which drives P. to his uncontrollable laughter? A partial answer naturally follows:

> scribimus inclusi, numeros ille, hic pede liber,
> grande aliquid quod pulmo animae praelargus anhelet.
> scilicet haec populo pexusque togaque recenti
> et natalicia tandem cum sardonyche albus
> sede leges celsa, liquido cum plasmate guttur
> mobile conlueris, patranti fractus ocello.

---

[18] Most edd. now agree that *cachinno* should be taken as a verb here rather than a noun.

> tunc neque more probo videas nec voce serena
> ingentis trepidare Titos, cum carmina lumbum
> intrant et tremulo scalpuntur ubi intima versu. (1.13-21)

Again we see here the persistent recurrence of the "inflation" theme. Over-inflated writers create massive (*grande*, 14) works requiring an enormous lung (*pulmo* ... *praelargus*, 14) to bellow out (*anhelet*, 14). There are also prevalent in 1.13-21 strongly implied references to effeminacy, *luxuria*, (pathic) homosexuality. Thus the perverse inflation of the poetasters' production is linked to their own perversion: their writing and performance reflect their lifestyle. Also of note is P.'s description of the (passive homosexual) reciter. He is clean and well groomed externally, yet internally he is corrupt. The description of his ornate birthday ring (*natalicia* ... *sardonyche*, 16) is not without purpose or merely incidental (cf., "what prompts the reciter to wear a birthday gift or why P. should draw attention to its being such is impossible to see.");[19] it is the mark of imposture and perversion, and it is duplicated by J. in a similar context (1.28-29, to vivify his portrayal of *luxuria*):

> ventilet aestivum digitis sudantibus aurum
> nec sufferre queat maioris pondera gemmae.

P.'s programmatic format retains and plays off the imaginary adversary. This technique imparts to the satire's progression a spontaneous levity which is absent in J. 1. J. instead invites the reader to identify with him and to share his indignation; he does so by juxtaposing the views of his internal voice with specific absurdities, thereby placing the reader on the side of the satirist. In contrast, P.'s adversary-technique causes the reader to shift repeatedly between two points of view--faults are enumerated by the satirist, the program is developed, and then the adversary interrupts with "objective" (in the sense that the adversary's remarks direct the aim of the discourse) commentary. This

---

[19] Harvey (1981) 21. Cf. also on the sardonyx (ring) J. 7.140 (... *nisi fulserit anulus ingens*); 7.143-44 (*Paulus agebat/sardonyche*).

in effect allows P. to draw out his *apologia* and at the same time gradually to *convince* the reader that his attacks are just.

In contrast, the following passage illustrates well J.'s technique of reader identification:

> difficile est saturam non scribere. nam quis iniquae
> tam patiens urbis, tam ferreus, ut teneat se,
> causidici nova cum veniat lectica Mathonis
> plena ipso, post hunc magni delator amici
> et cito rapturus de nobilitate comesa
> quod superest, quem Massa timet, quem munere palpat
> Carus et a trepido Thymele summissa Latino;
> cum te summoveant qui testamenta merentur
> noctibus, in caelum quos evehit optima summi
> nunc via processus, vetulae vesica beatae? (1.30-39)

After declaring that it is "difficult not to write satire," J. asks the rhetorical question, "Who is so steeled, so tolerant of unbalanced Rome, that he can restrain himself (from indignation)?" The implication is of course that *no one* is, and thus sides are drawn; it is we and J. against absurdity. And our identification is developed further at 1.37: it is *you* who are being pushed aside by gigolos. Also, we see here again imagery of fatness and consuming appetite: *lectica Mathonis/plena ipso* (32-33), and *rapturus de nobilitate comesa/quod superest* (34-35). Vice threatens to "snatch up" what remains of illustriousness (itself already "chewed up").[20]

But to return once more now to the programmatic development of P: whereas J. incorporates in his development exempla of malignant absurdity drawn from "real" life (e.g., *lectica Mathonis*, 1.32; *delator amici*, 1.33, etc.), P. retains his emphasis on letters and learning (as reflection of diseased morality). At 1.22-25 we are presented with P.'s adversary's[21] protest that study should naturally yield (poetic) release:

> tun, vetule, auriculis alienis colligis escas,

---

[20] Food as metaphor/marker of Roman satire is present from Lucilius through J. More on this will be presented in Chapter 3.

[21] Some edd. (e.g., Bo, [1969] 17) assign this question to the *poeta vetulus* of the preceding verses.

> articulis quibus et dicas cute perditus "ohe"?
> "quo didicisse, nisi hoc fermentum et quae semel intus
> innata est rupto iecore exierit caprificus?"

The metaphor naturally is arranged by P. so as to parody (by irony) bad writers' wonted claim to poetic inspiration. And the point is developed further in P.'s response:

> scire tuum nihil est nisi te scire hoc sciat alter? (1.27)

In short, implies P., "learning" need not imply worthwhile production; it will often result in mere perpetuation of pretentiousness:

> hic aliquis, cui circum umeras hyacinthina laena est,
> rancidulum quiddam balba de nare locutus
> Phyllidas, Hypsipylas, vatum et plorabile siquid,
> eliquat ac tenero subplantat verba palato. (1.32-35)

J. too utilizes the "bursting liver" (seat of [perverse] passion) metaphor to attack the producers of irrelevant and self-indulgent poetry, but transfers it out of his program piece and into *Satire* 7:

> rumpe miser tensum iecur, ut tibi lasso
> figantur virides, scalarum gloria, palmae. (7.117-118)

And the reference here is transferred to pleaders in court, whose inspiration is rooted in monetary gain only. Indeed then J., like P., while allowing for the passionate outbursts not only of poets, but even of pleaders, recognizes the perverse source of this passion for eloquence; it is, in part at least, the expectation of money (cf. also again P.'s *venter* and *dolosi spes nummi*, *Prol.*). This is not to say, however, that this desire for monetary gain is for either J. or P. the sole symptom of societal corruption. Rather, it is part of a more wide-ranging general corruption. Other indicators of this wider-ranging corruption are evident in P.1 especially. Note in this brief passage the desire for status on the part of P.'s pretentious poetaster:

> "at pulchrum est digito monstrari et dicier 'hic est.'
> ten cirratorum centum dictata fuisse
> pro nihilo pendes?" (1.28-30)

The desire for sexual recognition on the poetaster's part likewise is made manifest throughout P.1. Note for example 1.19-21:

> tunc neque more probo videas nec voce serena
> ingentis trepidare Titos, cum carmina lumbum
> intrant et tremulo scalpuntur ubi intima versu.

And finally, the desire for societal power facilitates corruption, hindering truthfulness and promoting hypocrisy. P.'s interlocutor reveals this perverse consciousness:

> "sed quid opus teneras mordaci radere vero
> auriculas? vide sis ne maiorum tibi forte
> limina frigescant: sonat hic de nare canina
> littera." (1.107-110)

3. *Indignationis Materia:* The Satirists' Wrath Schematized

P. protracts his assault on poetasters. After his adversary's next protest (*"rides,"* ait, "*et nimis uncis/naribus indulges,*" 1.40-41), he then combines his defense with a renewed attack on those (poets) who profess to love truth, but seek mere flattery. Here P. uses as his defense a reminiscence of his prologue (i.e., denial of poetic inspiration), and simultaneously admits that he is neither immune to praise nor made of (unfeeling) horn, the effect of which is to personalize the narrative, drawing us toward empathetic relation to the satirist:

> non ego, cum scribo, si forte quid aptius exit
> (quando haec rara avis est), si quid tamen aptius exit,
> laudari metuam; neque enim mihi cornea fibra est. (1.45-47)

And here begins his renewed assault:

> sed recti finemque extremumque esse recuso
> "euge" tuum et "belle." nam "belle" hoc excute totum:
> quid non intus habet? non hic est Ilias Atti
> ebria veratro? non siqua elegidia crudi
> dictarunt proceres? non quidquid denique lectis
> scribitur in citreis? calidum scis ponere sumen,
> scis comitem horridulum trita donare lacerna,
> et "verum," inquis, "amo, verum mihi dicite de me."
> qui pote? vis dicam? nugaris, cum tibi, calve,
> pinguis aqualiculus propenso sesquipede extet. (1.48-57)

Finally at this juncture P. brings his "turgidity" (fatness) theme directly into contact with its original embodiment (the connection thus far has only been implied; here it is realized). P.'s poetaster (who now evidently has assumed the identity of the adversary) is called directly babbling, bald, with a grotesquely enormous belly (the rather bizarre *aqualiculus* emphasizing the swinish deformity of the poetaster). Further, *crudi*, "raw," and *sumen*, 51, 53, hint at a metaphorical theme/image involving food, an image which will recur in P. (and which will be examined in Chapter 3).

J., in turn, after a short confirmation of his distaste of *captatores* (1.40-44), returns to his programmatic declaration of *indignatio*. But the *ira/indignatio* theme has by now been developed to the point that J. resorts to a quasi-rhetorical *praeteritio*; he need no longer express in detail with how much anger he seethes, yet he proceeds to enumerate its particular causes:

> quid referam quanta siccum iecur ardeat ira,
> cum populum gregibus comitum premit hic spoliator
> pupilli prostantis ... (1.45-47)

And immediately thereafter J. combines closely within a few verses three distinct (programmatic) themes, i.e., those of *avaritia*, the appeal to satiric precedent, and a renewed attack on contemporary poetry:

> ... quid enim salvis infamia nummis?
> exul ab octava Marius bibit et fruitur dis
> iratis, at tu victrix, provincia ploras.
> haec ego non credam Venusina digna Lucerna?
> haec ego non agitem? sed quid magis? Heracleas
> aut Diomedeas aut mugitum labyrinthi
> et mare percussum puero fabrumque volantem,
> cum leno accipiat moechi bona ... (1.48-55)

Indeed, the above verses are of large programmatic significance. Greed and private indulgence allow some (e.g., *Marius,* 49) unholy enjoyment (*dis/iratis*, 49-50) at the expense of the Empire, the image of Horace at his nocturnal satirizing is revived, again traditional mythological themes are sarcastically and disparagingly treated (the Minotaur is a mere *mugitum,* 53, Icarus an anonymous *puer*, Daedalus the "flying smith") and, perhaps of greatest import, the diverse ills of the private Roman microcosm have eclipsed the macrocosm of universal mythology (e.g., *leno ... moechi bona*, 55).

P.'s program continues to retain as its main emphasis the decline of poetry as *reflective* of moral decadence (in contrast to J., whose linkage of poor literature to poor general morality is relatively seamless). P. does, however, expand his criticism to the indefinite *populus:*

> 'quis populi sermo est?' (1.63)

P.[22] then replies:

---

[22] Clausen's attribution of lines to speakers at 1.63-65 is most likely wrong. Harvey (1981) 34: "63-65 (*quis ... unguis*) are spoken by P."

> ... quis enim nisi carmina molli
> nunc demum numero fluere, ut per leve severos
> ecfundat iunctura unguis? (1.63-65)

And criticism of the larger society is thus (re)introduced to the program; the *populi sermo*, 63 (which recalls *turbida Roma*, 5), proves to be invalid (it too lacks the ability to make sound literary judgements). Society cites as the marks of a good poet the ability to compose an even verse and to treat diverse literary *topoi*:

> ... scit tendere versum
> non secus ac si oculo rubricam derigat uno.
> sive opus in mores, in luxum, in prandia regum
> dicere, res grandes nostro dat Musa poetae. (1.65-68)

Yet in reality (and in recollection of the ineptitude of the contemporary poets as put forth in the beginning of the program), P. asserts, those of whom the *populus* approves are accustomed only to trifle (*nugari solitos Graece*, 1.70); common and easy themes are even beyond their ability, ... *nec ponere lucum*, 1.70. And notably, the public asserts that the Muse will provide the poet with grand themes, *res grandes*, 68, the very thing to which, it will be recalled, J. too objects especially at his program's outset (1.1-13). Thus better than half of P.'s program deals almost entirely with literature in decline and its attendant moral decadence. At 1.85 an issue which appears to be drawn from the larger sphere of "real" life is finally introduced (cf. J., who begins this at 1.22), yet this issue also is concerned with superficiality, affectation, and insincerity. Here the perversion of literature which P. has described is transferred to the realm of justice, and thus P. comes closer to meeting J. on another common theme: civilization as *victim* of its own moral insensibility. Justice is travestied by perverse poetic persuasiveness:

> "fur es," ait Pedio. Pedius quid? crimina rasis
> librat in antitithetis, doctas posuisse figuras
> laudatur: "bellum hoc." hoc bellum? an, Romule, ceves? (1.85-87)

The attribution to Romulus (who perhaps represents the court officials) of pathic effeminacy of course recalls 1.15-23 especially.

J.'s next programmatic appeal is interjected between descriptions of ostentatious youth (*puer Automedon*, 61), and unjustly acquired *luxuria* (*nam sexta cervice feratur ... signator falsi*, 64-67). It comes at 1.63, and is phrased in such a manner so as to demand compact with the reader:

> nonne libet medio ceras inplere capaces
> quadrivio ...

Ceras capaces, "vast tablets," appropriately is set up in answer to the overwhelming (vast) body of vice and corruption which J. has already particularized. Thus his program calls for a massive assault on massive corruption, perversity. *Nonne* of course expects a positive answer to the question posed; thus J. continues to draw the reader into sympathy with his own indignant state of mind, a technique singularly characteristic of his own program and not as well developed in that of P. (who, as we will see, prefers to insult and exclude deliberately those readers with whom he is not on sympathetic terms).

Also particularly noteworthy in J.'s programmatic development is what one might term "vivid vignettes." The reader, after having been confronted with the corruption of an imposingly massive collective corpus of absurdity, is presented with a series of vividly drawn pictures composed of exempla of corruption, vice in action (the vignette-technique is of course facilitated by the image of one standing at the crossroads, *quadrivio*, 64). Thus it is as though the reader feels himself being passed and surrounded by various personifications of corruption--personifications which are diligently perpetuating themselves even as we observe them. Consider one such vignette, and notice e.g., the (vivid) present tense and primary position of the initial verb, *occurrit*, and the vividly prospective *porrectura*:

> occurrit matrona potens, quae molle Calenum
> porrectura viro miscet sitiente rubetam
> instituitque rudes melior Lucusta propinquas
> per famam et populum nigros efferre maritos. (1.69-72)

And, probably in order not to enter prematurely into his satire proper, J., after a brief declaration that social mobility at Rome stems from crime (1.73-78), introduces what are arguably his most salient programmatic statements:

> si natura negat, facit indignatio versum
> qualemcumque potest, quales ego vel Cluvienus.[23]
> ex quo Deucalion nimbis tollentibus aequor
> navigio montem ascendit sortesque poposcit
> paulatimque anima caluerunt mollia saxa
> et maribus nudas ostendit Pyrrha puellas,
> quidquid agunt homines, votum, timor, ira, voluptas,
> gaudia, discursus, nostri farrago libelli est. (1.79-86)

These lines need little comment. J.'s satires will deal with vice, corruption, absurdity from the beginning of human existence through to the present; J. will trace their development, which is now at its fullest (*et quando uberior vitiorum copia?*, 87), and indeed J. fulfills this part of his program quite completely (cf. e.g., *Credo pudicitiam Saturno rege moratam ... at Satire* 6.1ff.). Yet there is in J.'s words a slight, yet remarkable, contradiction. The phrase *quidquid agunt homines*, 85, implies a universal program, but J.'s satiric picture is of course far from universal.[24]

J. 1.88-113 amounts to an extended divergence from the program which presents certain exempla of the themes of *avaritia, inhumanitas, luxuria*.[25] The theme of *avaritia* is

---

[23] About this Cluvienus, unfortunately nothing certain is known (his significance therefore is really lost to us). Re. Cluvienus, the most recent commentary on J., Courtney (1980), merely repeats select material gleaned from earlier commentators, e.g., Mayor (1877); Courtney 102 may be correct, however, in suggesting that Cluvienus is "clearly some poetaster."

[24] This aspect is noted also by Green (1974) 23: "But in fact this programme is never carried out. Juvenal writes from a very limited viewpoint, and the traverse of his attack is correspondingly narrow." To delete verses 1. 85-86 (as some commentators have advised) would of course impart to J.'s words a less universal programmatic tone.

[25] These three abstractions are all of one 'race;' they are complementary entities. Mayor (1877) 131 even perceives here certain personifications: "*avaritia*, like *alea* here and *gula* 140n., is personified; she opens wide the folds of her *toga* to receive." Cf. for P.'s personifications of *Avaritia* and *Luxuria* 5.132ff.

introduced first, and it is likened by J. to a creature with a "gaping" *sinus* (88).[26] *Alea*, "gaming," 88, follows naturally the introduction of *avaritia*:

> quando
> maior avaritiae patuit sinus? alea quando
> hos animos? neque enim loculis comitantibus itur
> ad casum tabulae, posita sed luditur arca. (1.87-90)

Inhumanitas is suggested immediately thereafter by:

> simplexne furor sestertia centum
> perdere et horrenti tunicam non reddere servo? (1.92-3)

And finally (present-day) *luxuria* is exemplified, contrasted with the simplicity of time past (that of one's "grandfather"):

> quis totidem erexit villas, quis fercula septem
> secreto cenavit avus? (1.94-5)

The digression of 1.88-113 allows J. to introduce *funesta Pecunia* as the reigning Roman "deity." And those positive abstractions of *Pax, Fides, Victoria, Virtus*, and *Concordia* (115-16), while ostensibly set up by J. in contrast to *Pecunia*, actually serve as antitheses to the ills which have been touched upon thus far in the larger satiric program: *Pax* recalls its perverted oppositions symbolized by *proelia quanta videbis* (91, refering to the "warfare" of the gaming table); *vincant divitiae* (110) points up the civil strife caused by greed. *Fides* is betrayed by a *magni delator amici* (33), *spoliator pupilli* (46-47), *signator falsi* (67), and by avaricious mendacity, *falso nomine poscas* (98). *Victoria* desecrated laments: *at tu victrix, provincia, ploras* (50). Humanity and *Virtus*

---

[26] *Sinus* here is generally taken by edd. simply as "pocket," or "fold of a garment." Equally attractive and applicable (in accord with *avaritia*'s personification) are these other meanings of *sinus*: "embrace," "nurturing bosom," (cf. 7.112; 6.607 where *Fortuna improba* personified takes *infantes* to her breast); "purse" (strengthening imagery of greed); even "cavity," *sensu obsceno* (see Adams [1982] 90 for *sinus* as "vagina" in e.g., Tibullus, Ovid); thus the possible image of a whorish *Avaritia* with "gaping vagina." This image too complements that of *uberior*, 1.87, where the root *uber* implies a bloated teat. J. may also imply that *avaritia* is like a ship in full "sail;" cf. his use of *sinus* in this sense at 1.150. *Sinus* is also used by J. to signify "net" at 4.41; it is easy to imagine a "net of avarice." But the passage profits from the ambiguity of *sinus*: one may imagine any or all of the above connotations.

have vanished: *tener uxorem ducat spado* (22); *probitas laudatur et alget* (74); *praetextatus adulter* (78); *tunicam non reddere servo* (93). And finally, greed has driven people apart and erased *Concordia*: *criminibus debent hortos, praetoria, mensas ...* (75); household union has been shattered, *leno accipiat moechi bona* (55); family fortunes are squandered, *caret omni maiorum censu* (59-60); wives even murder husbands, *matrona ...viro miscet sitiente rubetam* (69-70). Yet the predominace of *avaritia* in the program is maintained; *Pax, Fides, Victoria, Virtus, Concordia* are *all* overshadowed and contaminated by it.

P.'s program naturally contains far fewer explicit references to *avaritia* than does that of J. Nevertheless, it is a theme hinted at by P. in, for example, the picture of the (shipwrecked) sailor who "sings" his misery. In short, P.'s sailor is an impostor, his ruse having been prepared the night before, and the fact of his singing reveals insincerity:

>men moveat? quippe et, cantet si naufragus, assem
>protulerim? cantas, cum fracta te in trabe pictum
>ex umero portes? verum, nec nocte paratum,
>plorabit qui me volet incurvasse querella. (1.88-91)

And the idea that (avaricious) insincerity can be (and often is) glossed over by pseudo-grandiloquence (such as that of the *naufragus*) is not yet admitted by P.'s adversary, who continues to display critical inability:

>"sed numeris decor est et iunctura addita crudis.
>cludere sic versum didicit 'Berecyntius Attis'
>et 'qui caeruleum dirimebat Nerea delphin,'
>sic 'costam longo subduximus Appennino.'
>'Arma virum,' nonne hoc spumosum et cortice pingui
>ut ramale vetus vegrandi subere coctum?" (1.92-97)[27]

---

[27] Most edd. now agree that 96-97 should be attributed to the adversary and not to P. Ramsay (1918), who attributes 96-98 to P., turns *Arma virum* (96) into an exclamation: "O shade of Virgil!", but this is both semantically forced and critically unnecessary. *Berecyntius Attis* (93), *caeruleum ... delphin* (94), are evidently Ovidian conflations (see Harvey [1981] 44). *Costam ... Appennino* (95) has not been traced to any source; cf. Bo 29, "ex quo carmine versus afferatur incertum est neque facile est dictu quid significet." On *Attis*, however, see Lee and Barr (1987) 79-80. It may be that P.'s *Attis* reference is designed to disparage conscious imitators of Catullus and/or Ovid (cf. Lee and Barr, who cite Cat. 63, Ovid, *F.* 4221ff.); likewise, there may be implied an attack on Neronian Callimacheanism.

The self-defacing irony of P.'s adversary is manifest here. His "decorous" lines involve complicated metaphors, yet he accuses the simple *Arma virum* of frothiness and excessive padding. But P. cajoles his adversary further:

> quidnam igitur tenerum et laxa cervice legendum? (1.98)

The resulting quasi-Catullan[28] verses give P. the opportunity finally to disparage directly self-indulgent treatments of mythical themes:

> 'torva Mimalloneis inplerunt cornua bombis,
> et raptum vitulo caput ablatura superbo
> Bassaris et Lyncem Maenas flexura corymbis
> euhion ingeminat, reparabilis adsonat echo.'
> haec fierent si testiculi vena ulla paterni
> viveret in nobis? summa delumbe saliva
> hoc natat in labris et in udo est Maenas et Attis
> nec pluteum caedit nec demorsos sapit unguis. (1.99-106)

The emphases in P.'s attack on his adversary's literary exempla involve two aspects: 1) the nervelessness (effeminacy) and pretentiousness of these verses and 2) their unoriginality (they are uninspired, since their author has not moiled over them). This provides the overall Persian program with nothing fresh. What is important, however, about P.'s explicit criticism here is that it leads to a programmatic attempt (by the adversary) to dissuade the satirist from writing material which will offend; and this is complemented by P.'s defense and appeal to Lucilius and Horace. As we will see, J. too, in a quite similar fashion, develops a *dissuasio* only to follow it with a rebuttal.

---

[28] On the Catullan nature of 1.99-106 see again Lee and Barr (1987) 81-82, where a comparison is drawn with Cat: 64.254-64. Re. 1.99-102 Lee and Barr also note P.'s possible attack on Nero('s verse).

4. *Dissuasionis Reiectio:* The Satirists Commit Themselves

Here P. has his adversary warn against impudence:

> 'sed quid opus teneras mordaci radere vero
> auriculas? vide sis ne maiorum tibi forte
> limina frigescant: sonat hic de nare canina
> littera.' (1.107-110)

P. responds immediately with sarcasm. His program has already demonstrated poetic and moral decadence and its concomitant critical hypocrisy. And by now the adversary too realizes that P.'s criticisms are true (*mordaci radere vero*, 107). *Sonat hic de nare canina/littera* (109-110) is ambiguous and, taken one way provides greater programmatic significance than if taken in the other. Virtually all editors attribute these words to the adversary, and this seems correct given the abrupt response (of P.'s primary satiric persona): *per me equidem sint omnia protinus alba* (110). The first meaning of *sonat ... littera* is complementary to the idea that a satirist might be excluded from the "thresholds of the great;" naturally, a snarling response might be expected from a satire's victim. But, in accordance with another way P. may have intended the phrase (more programmatically significant also) would be to construe *sonat ... littera* as self-reflexive [i.e., the "dog-letter," or growling speech, refers to the practice of satirizing ("scraping tender little ears with caustic truth"); thus *hic* at 109 depends not on *limina*, but rather refers to P.'s *cynical* poetry]. And of course the satiric tradition might be recalled here by P. to its roots in Cynicism.[29]

Here then is how P. responds first to his adversary's *dissuasio* against writing satire:

> nil moror. euge omnes, omnes bene, mirae eritis res.
> hoc iuvat? 'hic,' inquis, 'veto quisquam faxit oletum.'
> pinge duos anguis: 'pueri, sacer est locus, extra
> meiite.' discedo. (1.111-114)

---

[29] Cf. e.g., A. Gellius, *Noctes Atticae* 2.18.7: *Ex quibus ille Menippus fuit cuius libros M. Varro in satiris aemulatus est, quas alii "Cynicas," ipse appellat "Menippeas."* and 13.31(30).1: ... <u>Saturarum</u> *M. Varronis enarrator, quas partim Cynicas, alii Menippeas appellant.*

Thus P. pretends for the time being to take his adversary's warning seriously; he jokingly compares himself to a mischievous *puer*. Line 111 is of course purely sarcastic. *Euge omnes, omnes bene* recalls the flattery given poor poets earlier in the satire (cf. e.g., 53: *'euge' tuum et 'belle.'*; 75: *euge poeta!*). The ground over which P. would spread his satire is likened to a sacred region wherein no impure imposition is allowed. This is of course ironic, and leads to P.'s ironic, *discedo*. But his "yielding" is halted by an invocatory recollection of the originator of the satiric tradition:

> secuit Lucilius urbem,
> te Lupe, te Muci, et genuinum fregit in illis. (1.114-15)

Horace too maintained this tradition, was not dissuaded from pointing out society's faults, and thus P. is inspired to do likewise (further, the appeal to these earlier satirists serves to validate P.'s own *apologia*):

> omne vafer vitium ridenti Flaccus amico
> tangit et admissus circum praecordia ludit,
> callidus excusso populum suspendere naso. (1.116-18)

Thus, given the examples of Lucilius and Horace, asks P., why should he be denied like liberty of expression:

> me muttire nefas? nec clam? nec cum scrobe? nusquam?
> hic tamen infodiam. vidi, vidi ipse libelle:
> auriculas asini quis non habet? hoc ego opertum,
> hoc ridere meum, tam nil, nulla tibi vendo
> Iliade. (1.119-23)

Here P. declares that he will indeed confide, at least to his *libellus*, his secret: all men have the (little) ears of an ass. And this is, in P.'s view, an insight more profound than what can be discovered in the largest epic. There may also of course be an ironic reminiscence of Catullus 1.1 (*cui dono lepidum novum libellum*), the irony being that P. understands the "real" (i.e. satiric) Catullus, unlike the pseudo-neoterics of Neronian Rome. Of note here also is P.'s ostensible assessment of his satire (*ridere meum*) as insignificant (*tam nil*); neither will it be sold (cf. the mercenary theme of the prologue especially); and *Iliade* recalls Labeo (1.1.4), who would of course aspire to sell his epic translations.

Before J. presents his programmatic *dissuasio* and rebuttal, he elaborates further on what are essentially three distinct, yet complementary themes: greed, the inferior lifestyle of the dependent client, and *luxuria* (exemplified by excessive consumption of food). These elaborations can be quite precisely distinguished as follows: greed (which follows directly the introduction of *funesta Pecunia*) is demonstrated at 1.116-26; the client's daily struggle at 127-34; *luxuria* and excessive appetite at 135-46. And each of these themes, while still in accord with J.'s program thus far, will indeed be taken up in the satires which follow. Most notably, greed is dealt with in *Satires* 9 (homosexuals are mercenary with their favors), 10, 12 (actually an admonition against greed), and 14 (where parents are said actually to *teach* their children *avaritia*). The tribulations of the struggling client are dealt with especially in 3 (Umbricius' exodus from Rome is motivated primarily by his inability to rise to a higher socio-economic level), 4, and 5 (the patron treats his clients very poorly at dinner). Excessive eating furnishes a thematic cornerstone in 4, 5, and 11. The resemblance of J. 1.142-146 to P. 3.98-106 has already been mentioned. J. includes the picture of the gourmand dying in the bath in his program, rather than elsewhere, most likely because it ties in so appropriately with the description of the hungry client (the theme of which recurs frequently in other satires); thus the prominent contrast between *lassi clientes* (132) and *quanta ... gula* (140).

At 1.147 J. finally begins to develop his *dissuasio* and defense. Every vice, he asserts, is now at its highest point; posterity could not possibly furnish further iniquity. Thus he will "spread sail" and embark on his voyage against absurdity:

> nil erit ulterius quod nostris moribus addat
> posteritas, eadem facient cupientque minores,
> omne in praecipiti vitium stetit: utere velis,
> totos pande sinus. (1.147-50)

Thus J. is asserting that if there is ever a time when satire should be justly undertaken, there is no time so appropriate as his own. Nevertheless, a programmatic *dissuasio* follows, introducing not a fictive interlocutor, but inviting the reader into the text:[30]

> dices hic forsitan "unde
> ingenium par materiae? unde illa priorum
> scribendi quodcumque animo flagrante liberet
> simplicitas?" (1.150-53)

Verses 153-54, J. (the satirist's) first response to the *dissuasio*, are remarkable for their similarity to P. 1.114-15:

> "cuius non audeo dicere nomen?
> quid refert dictis ignoscat Mucius an non?" (J. 1.153-54)

The Mucius mentioned here (and by P. at 1.115) is the P. Mucius Scaevola satirized by Lucilius, but he has now become no less than a programmatic symbol of vice.[31] The Mucius-exemplum is expanded and the potential punishment of the satirist expressed vividly:

> pone Tigellinum, taeda lucebis in illa
> qua stantes ardent qui fixo guttere fumant,
> *   *   *   *   *   *
> et latum media sulcum deducit harena." (1.155-57)[32]

The point stressed here is that the castigators of criminals will themselves be punished severely, an idea which is entirely absent from the Persian program (P.'s adversary warns only that a satirist might be excluded from the doors of the eminent). But to abstain from exposing crime and vice is naturally unacceptable to J.:

> qui dedit ergo tribus patruis aconita, vehatur

---

[30] Of course what follows 1.150 could be described (Ferguson [1979] 123) thus: "J. imagines himself objecting to his own commission: a kind of internal dialogue follows." But the reader's involvement in the program must not be discounted; the second person (e.g., *dices*) does indeed retain the interpersonal fiber of the discourse. J. is speaking to "himself," the reader, and any potential satirist.

[31] Evidently J. actually quoted Lucilius here, just as P. did at 1.1. J. is in fact cited as the source for this verse in collections of Lucilius' fragments (see e.g., Krenkel [1970] 720).

[32] Re. these verses cf. Clausen (1959) 42, "post 156 unum versum excidisse censuit Housman."

> pensilibus plumis atque illinc despiciat nos? (1.158-59)

His satire must therefore emerge, yet in a veil. Blatant outspokeness, however slight, will be noticed:

> cum veniet contra, digito compesce labellum:
> accusator erit qui verbum dixerit "hic est." (160-61)[33]

As commentators point out,[34] J. returns to the theme that innocuous literary treatments can be published without even threat of injurious consequences. The purpose of stressing this here again is to underline the contrast between the satirist (the boldest of whom is of course embodied by Lucilius) and the unoriginal court poet. Note the acuity of juxtaposition where J. contrasts the vehement Lucilius with the exemplum of absolutely unoffensive stock mythological themes:

> securus licet Aenean Rutulumque ferocem
> committas, nulli gravis est percussus Achilles
> aut multum quaesitus Hylas urnamque secutus:
> ense velut stricto quotiens Lucilius ardens
> infremuit, rubet auditor cui frigida mens est
> criminibus, tacita sudant praecordia culpa. (1.162-67)

It has been supposed that J., in referring to *percussus Achilles*, is deliberately recalling the work of Statius[35] who, although publishing and proclaiming during the reign of Domitian, evidently never incurred his displeasure. It is quite possible, however, since

---

[33] An argument could be made for reading *verum* at 1.161 in place of *verbum*. This would not only eliminate the slight problem created by the two-word expression "*hic est*," but would also recall the similar usage by P. at 1.107: *mordaci radere vero/auriculas?* Cf. Clausen's apparatus (42): verbum *man. recentior in P, codd. Vallae*: versum *PR*: versu *V*: verum Φ. *cf. Pers.* i. 107. Further, Φ actually represents many and diverse codd.

[34] E.g., Ferguson (1979) 124. J. terminates his program with a recollection of its inception. Ferguson: "Notice how J uses 'ring form': we are back to the mythical poems of the beginning."

[35] Sic Ferguson (1979) 124: "But J has in mind the fact that P. Papinius Statius (AD 45-96) was able to write an *Achilleis* under Domitian without losing the favor of the court, though he died a natural death before reaching the end of Achilles's life." Yet J.'s citation of the *Theseid* of the "unknown" (Ferguson 111) Cordus (1.2) evidently refers not to a significant (well known) work, but rather is used by J. as an exemplum of an irrelevant, trite literary *topos*; but its author is named. Statius is named by J. at 7.83 only, and his *Achilleis* is not made reference to, but rather his *Thebais*. The other instances in which J. mentions Achilles (7.210, 8.271, 10.256, 11.30, 14.214) do not imply an *Achilleis* at all, but rather involve Achilles as a Homeric (mythological) signifier of heroic *statura*.

Statius' *Achilleis* ended before the hero actually became *percussus*, that J. did not have Statius' work in mind especially. Achilles (and Hylas) may simply be representative of trite mythological literary themes. The point, at any rate, is that a poet (of J.'s day) may write on such themes while remaining *securus* (162); the prototypical satirist, on the other hand, roared (*infremuit*) and, burning with anger (*ardens*), attacked individuals as though with sword drawn (*ense velut stricto*). And this is J.'s definite preference: to separate himself from the crowd of poets who treat common themes and to strike out honestly and cynically against reality.

J.'s next assertion, which leads to a final admonition against writing satire, is ambiguous; *inde ira et lacrimae* (168) can be interpreted in two ways, and it is unclear which way J. originally intended it (or if the ambiguity was deliberate). Virtually all editors cite here a parallel expression from Terence's *Andria*.[36] But Ferguson[37] confirms the more apparent interpretation: "*Ira* is the guilty man's, *lacrimae* the poet's." Yet, we might suggest, *ira* can refer to the (programmatic) anger and *indignatio* of the satirist in general (J. has just described Lucilius as "raging"), and *inde ira et lacrimae* would therefore complement the *dissuasio* which begins in the same line; thus, "Whence [comes] anger, [so come] tears." Indeed, this interpretation seems the better suited to the admonitory nature of this passage (1.165-71). The message imparted is then that rage (*ira*), if expressed (as Lucilius'), results in punishment (*lacrimae*) for the satirist. And the rest of the admonition (*dissuasio*) follows up on this idea naturally:

>   'tecum prius ergo voluta
> haec animo ante tubas: galeatum sero duelli
> paenitet.' (1.168-70)

---

[36] E.g., Weidner (1889) 20: "Anspielung auf ein bekanntes Wort des Ter. Andr. 126 hinc illae lacrumae ..." Later edd. reiterate.

[37] Ferguson (1979) 124.

And finally J., in ostensible acquiescence to the *dissuasio*, declares that he will try what is allowed only against the dead. This declaration, however, while true in part (J. does indeed satirize figures of the past), is of course not only a cynical comment on current life at Rome (there is no true freedom of speech), but is also a way of masking his attacks on contemporary persons. Yet too there is irony here, since J. overtly professes to opt for the "art of safe speaking," just as did the epicists whom he criticizes.

P., in marked contrast to J., ends his program not with a *dissuasio*/admonition, but with another limitation of his potential audience.[38] Thus he, like J., returns at the close of his satire to recall the beginning. P. lays as much stress on the kind of reader he wants to exclude as he does on the kind he prefers to include. His desire to have a reader who studies Old Comedy recalls, and is probably based on, Horace:[39]

> audaci quicumque adflate Cratino
> iratum Eupolidem praegrandi cum sene palles,[40]
> aspice et haec, si forte aliquid decoctius audis. (1.123-25).

Thus P. confirms the connection between (his) Roman Satire and Attic Old Comedy. The outspoken criticism of contemporary personages and events is by implication what P. promises therefore. And he requires for this material a *lector* with a "steam-cleaned"

---

[38] Lee and Barr (1987) 86 call this practice "commonplace," and cite Lucilius 632-635 *ROL*, Hor. *Serm.* 1.4.73 and 1.10.81ff. Indeed, in marked contrast to P. is J.'s apparent absence of overt concern about a readership (audience).

[39] At *Serm.* 1.4.1, Horace likewise lists Eupolis, Cratinus, Aristophanes as poets who would censure openly a *malus, fur, moechus*, or *sicarius*, and states further: *hinc omnis pendet Lucilius* (1.4.6. Lee and Barr's citation errs slightly).

[40] The somewhat perplexing *palles* is discussed by Harvey (1981) 52; indeed, why a reader should "pale" at Old Comedy is not clear. It is therefore probably best to assume that both apparent possibilities apply: one might grow pale by fright (at Old Comedy's ferocity) or by passing long periods in reading Greek MSS, thus "the pallor of study" (Harvey 52). Cf. also P.'s use of *inpallescere* in this sense at 5.62: *at te nocturnis iuvat inpallescere chartis*. At 4.47 P. uses *palles* for one who catches sight of money; there it implies emotional instability.

ear.[41] Likewise, P. excludes expressly from his readership the base-humored (*sordidus*), whose laughter is aroused by such simple-minded amusements as odd shoes or facial mutilation:

> non hic qui in crepidas Graiorum ludere gestit
> sordidus et lusco qui possit dicere "lusce." (1.127-28)

And, in a description replicated by J., P. excludes the self-important pseudo-aristocrat:

> sese aliquem credens Italo quod honore supinus
> fregerit heminas Arreti aedilis iniquas. (1.129-30)

Commentators do not explain what specifically P. may have been stressing here.[42] J. 10.100-102 is interwoven into a larger context (encompassing the theme that excessive honor or wealth are sought without consideration of their consequences), and therefore serves to elucidate the meaning of P.'s passage:

> huius qui trahitur praetextam sumere mavis
> an Fidenarum Gabiorumque esse potestas
> et de mensura ius dicere, vasa minora
> frangere pannosus vacuis aedilis Ulubris? (J. 10.99-102)

The *aedilis* of J. and the official *sese aliquem credens* of P. are typical of anyone who, although currently "big fish in small ponds," seek recognition not only beyond their due, but also beyond reason. In short, these persons represent foolish, although abusive, holders of insignificant office who pretend importance. And such types are by nature devoid of the slightest consciousness of a philosophically sound world-view. Politicians of this strain would have provided (and indeed did) perfect targets for Old Comedy; thus P.'s inclusion of this exemplum at this particular point in his program.

---

[41] K. Reckford (1962) 476ff. sees overwhelming programmatic significance in what he terms, "the key metaphor of diseased ears" re. P.1. P.'s ear-motif figures prominently in his philosophical message, as will be seen in Chapter 4.

[42] One exception is Bo (1969) 36; he says very little, however: 'sese magnum virum credens' to illucidate *sese aliquem credens*, hardly a notable observation.

Likewise, the anti-intellectual whose study amounts to "laughing at" mathematical calculations and geometric forms and whose commendation is attained by a playful girl who tugs a Cynic's beard, is not fit to appreciate P.'s satire:

> nec qui abaco numeros et secto in pulvere metas
> scit risisse vafer,[43] multum gaudere paratus
> si cynico barbam petulans nonaria vellat. (1.131-33)

The last line of P.'s program is singularly problematic:

> his mane edictum, post prandia Callirhoen do. (1.134)[44]

There is no need to repeat here the various speculations posited about *edictum* and *Callirhoen*. Whether the "edict" referred to by commentators here is that of the praetor or is a play-bill, and whether *Callirhoen* is a *meretrix* (of some renown) or is the title of a play, is evidently non-discernible. Given, however, the context of what precedes the final line of P.'s program, it is perhaps slightly more plausible to suggest that P. "gives" unworthy readers over to a list of plays in the morning, and suggests that in the afternoon they go to one of these (i.e., *Callirhoen*). Further, *Callirhoe* etymologically suggests (of verse perhaps) "fair-flowing (stream)," and may be in deliberate reference to the concern of the *populus* with "smooth-flowing" poetry. But beyond this lies P.'s outright dismissal of those undeserving of his satires. And this is the natural conclusion to the program. P. has demonstrated literary decadence, exemplified its manifestations, declared himself a satirist; his final execution is self-liberation by definition of readership.

J.'s programmatic conclusion is no less abrupt. It is posited as a response to the admonition:

> "tecum ergo prius voluta
> haec animo ante tubas: galeatum sero duelli
> paenitet." experiar quid concedatur in illos
> quorum Flaminia tegitur cinis atque Latina. (1.168-71)

---

[43] In commenting on *vafer*, it seems better to assert that it is simply ironic (in its usual sense of "artistic, skilled, clever, etc.") rather than synonymous with 'improbus' (sic Bo [1969] 36).

[44] Lee and Barr (1987) 87 note the comparable dismissal of unworthies at Hor. *Serm.* 1.10.90ff.

The epic language of *tecum ... paenitet*, is perhaps deliberately phrased by J. to recall those poets who only repeat trite (e.g., epic) themes.[45] Thus it is as though one such poet puts forth to J. the satirist this final *dissuasio*. The overtly military quality of these lines is also remarkable (e.g., *ante ... tubas*; *galeatum ... duelli*), since the implication follows that J. is (like Lucilius) about to embark on a "martial assault."[46]

The last line of J.'s program, rather unlike that of P., infers a concession to the *dissuasio*. Critics conjecture that J., by saying that he will "try" what is allowed against those who are buried beneath the Flaminian and Latin ways, indicates that the centers of his satires will be representative figures of the nobility (since this is where the tombs of the upper-classes were generally located). There may be some validity to this viewpoint, since J. does indeed criticize the nobility, but J. criticizes not only past nobility, but also contemporary.

Of note also is the final word of J.1. By its final position, *Latina* calls attention to itself and may have been designed to connect *Latina via* with *Latina lingua*. This is to suggest that J. will "uncover" what lies hidden not only beneath the Latin way, but he will also "expose" all else which seeks to remain buried in Latin (Roman) society. *Latina* itself suggests, furthermore, all that is essentially "Latin" (Roman): language, *mores*, values, beliefs, etc. (Contrast J.'s policy of exposure with P.'s desire to "bury" material

---

[45] Cf. Ferguson (1979) 124: "*voluta*: epic parody cf. Verg. *A* 4, 533, *secumque ita corde volutat*; 6, 157; 6, 185."

[46] Ferguson (1979) 124 also notes the obvious military imagery here. But in explaining *duelli* (169), Ferguson suggests: "archaic for *belli* (so that war originates as a 'duel'; cf *bis* from *duis*). But why does J use the archaism here? Probably to give his caution a kind of hieratic wisdom and religious validity." Ferguson thinks that J. suddenly, by the use of a single archaism, imparts a sacerdotal "wisdom" or "religious validity" to his program, an idea which fails to convince. The significance of the archaic language here is two-fold. First, the imaginary, or internal (to J.), adversary here couches his admonition in ante-classical vocabulary--this amounts to affected style, something which J. has already censured; thus the disparity is stressed here between this style and that of J. The "duel" idea implied in *duelli* therefore recalls the two factions already established by J., i.e., those of, on the one hand, us the readers in sympathy with J. the satirist, and, on the other hand, the collective body of vice, absurdity, etc. which has been set in opposition. Second, proverbial expressions (with which 1.168-70 is undoubtedly akin) were (and still are) often couched in archaic language.

and hide it in his *libellus*--P. professes to bury his secret, yet he reveals it anyway. This antithetical dichotomy of exposure and burial is an important manifestation of the difference in satiric approach between P. and J.). Thus J.'s declaration is two-stage, so to speak: overtly he will criticize only the famous dead; implicitly (and this is borne out) J. criticizes these famous dead as representatives of the (in)famous living.

In form, 1.170-71 are posited as an acknowledgement of the previous admonition. Yet indeed, as will be observed in Chapter 4, J. does, in apparent contradiction of 1.170-71, satirize figures who could be interpreted as representative of his contemporaries.[47]

---

[47] This was the view of some early edd. and has been repeated by more recent ones. See e.g., Weidner (1889) 20: "Übrigens verspricht Juv. mit dieser Bemerkung nicht etwa eine historische Satire, sondern er deutet an, dass er zur Shilderung der Zustände seiner Zeit, statt hervorragende Manner aus ihr zu wahlen, auf entsprechende Charaktere der jungst vergangenen Zeit zurückgreifen wolle."

CHAPTER 2

PERSONAE IN PERSIUS AND JUVENAL

1. Persian Paradox: *Unus Ait Comitum:* Admixture Of Voice

From the outset (*Prologue, Satire* 1) we have observed that P.'s poetry is paradoxical, experimental, original, defiant--petulant poetry, aimed at catalysis of traditional poesy. Although a self-conscious successor of Lucilius and Horace, P. has essentially redefined satiric composition, its unique nature now reflective of a peculiarly idiopathic Neronian (literary) society.

We see in P. 3 dissevered discourse--discourse dissevered in the sense that the narrative structure strikes the reader as non-sequential. The satire opens enigmatically--the initial statement, *Nempe haec adsidue*,1, defines no immediate dramatic context. Further, as we proceed with the satire, there arises a marked dilemma about the (various) voices which appear. That we as readers are at once perplexed is not accidental. Just as P. succeeded in his program in shattering the formalities of traditional poetic construction, so too if we expect to perceive a "personal" development which is uniform and consistent, identifiable and unambivalent, our expectation will be met with abrupt disintegration of the (expected) norm.

Toward *Satire* 3 much critical attention has been directed in an effort to resolve what strikes the reader as an incoherent mixture of voices.[1] This criticism has resulted in diverse punctuation of the text, with the concomitant result that the various editions differ notably in this respect.[2]

---

[1] For a brief summary of discussions of voice in P.3 (including that of Housman [1972]), see Lee and Barr (1987) 100-101.
[2] Indeed, by far the most revealing (and massive, affecting meaning) differences from Clausen's *OCT* involve for Lee and Barr (1987) *Sat.* 3. These edd. list (59) a total of nineteen modified lines of text (wherewith they differ from Clausen) in *Sat.* 3; cf. six for *Sat.* 1, two for *Sat.* 2, five for *Sat.* 4, thirteen for *Sat.* 5, and four for *Sat.* 6. Note also that *Sat.* 3 is by no means the longest of the satires.

In *Satire* 3 P. creates a (dramatic) setting wherein even the primary figure(s) is indefinite:

>   iam clarum mane fenestras
> intrat et angustas extendit lumine rimas.
> stertimus, indomitum quod despumare Falernum
> sufficiat, quinta dum linea tangitur umbra. (3.1-4)

This setting of late-morning repose is established only to be recast by the introduction of a sudden, even explosive, '*en quid agis?*', 5, followed by another (indefinite at this point) pastoral voice:

>   'siccas insana canicula messes
> iam dudum coquit et patula pecus omne sub ulmo est' (3.5-6)

As readers we are now impatient for clarification of this scene. P. provides it, but briefly and inexactly. A rather staccato series of questions (indefinite as to both their source and direction) follows only to be supplemented by another shift in voice (from first person plural to singular):

> unus ait comitum. 'verumne? itan? ocius adsit
> huc aliquis. nemon?' turgescit vitrea bilis:
> findor, ut Arcadiae pecuaria rudere credas. (3.7-9)

Findor now provides us with what seems a clue to the satirist's persona, the "I" of the drama, the narrator. And our narrator then initiates narrative, describing his activity as he is about to write; but P. again pre-empts our expectation and dissolves our burgeoning perception by reverting to another shift in perspective--the "I" disappears again in deference to *querimur* 12, 14, *venimus* 16:[3]

> iam liber et positis bicolor membrana capillis
> inque manus chartae nodosaque venit harundo.
> tum querimur crassus calamo quod pendeat umor.
> nigra sed infusa vanescit sepia lympha,

---

[3] Cf. J. Henderson (1989) 14-15 re. P.'s "theatre of language:" "... the voicing of the poetry crumbles and breaks up into morsels of discourse, quasi-somatic hunks. Roles are embryonic, inchoate. The pronominal network of 'I-You-We-They-Thou' mutates abruptly, short circuits. With these spin subject and object, agency and passivity, satirist and victim, self and other, Teacher and Pupil ...", indeed an apt and accurate assessment.

>   dilutas querimur geminat fistula guttas.
>   o miser inque dies ultra miser, hucine rerum
>   venimus? (3.10-16)

And subsequently (3.16) a voice emerges which will impugn, evidently, the sleeper/scribe; this is the *comes* of verse 7, and it is his opinions which generally overshadow those of the other voices in the satire. Thus the expected persona, the sleeper/scribe, is now essentially mere exemplum, providing the *comes* the opportunity to develop an animadversive caveat.[4] And, rather than making this caveat/criticism recipient-specific, P., by deliberately disarranging the nexus of voices, by creating sudden discourse uninterrupted by directional mandate, in which speakers change improvidently, succeeds in making the satire indefinite, yet at the same time individually pertinent; and, as the satire proceeds, the exemplum of the speaker/scribe is supplemented by those of the "goatish centurion" (*aliquis de gente hircosa centurionum,* 77), and the invalid (*qui dicit medico,* 90). Thus the satire presents an amalgam of voices, in turn creating a disjointed scene, its coherence dependent upon a subcurrent theme rather than a coherent and unifying persona.

It is at 3.19 that the voice (persona) of the censor finally emerges as predominant, there being only one final objection from what appears to be the sleeper/scribe: *an tali studeam calamo?*, 19. Verses 19-30 reveal a persona which directly impugns a second person (presumably again the sleeper/scribe, but certainly the criticism is directed at a more generic "you"). The voice of the censor tells us little about the character; he is aggressively offensive toward the "you" of the passage, and he justifies his verdict with the assertion that his perception is well founded (*ego te intus et in cute novi*, 30).

---

[4] It is of course oversimple to designate a definite and limited recipient of this *caveat*, or simply to assert that the biographical P. is identifiable as such. Cf. Lee and Barr (1987) 102 who do just this: "The use of the first person, whether singular, *findor*, or plural, *querimur* (12, 14), merely underlines the point that P. *qua* narrator is talking about himself *qua* the delinquent character in the drama."

Further, P. plies two antithetical personae: the one in need of (moral) correction, and the one whose purpose is to "shape" the recalcitrant just as a potter shapes clay:[5]

> udum et molle lutum es, nunc nunc properandus et acri
> fingendus sine fine rota. (3.23-4)

It is these contrasting personae which provide for the advancement of the satire, yet further exempla of antithetical representation (as regards the persona of the Stoic philosopher) are provided to add clarity to the drama. The *suasoria* consisting of verses 19 (*'cui verba ...'*) through 76, while keeping the voice of the Stoic censor at the fore, are nevertheless best construed as a dialogue, again involving the voice of the sleeper/scribe (who speaks vv. 44-51). It follows logically (although this is no guarantee of P.'s intent), then, that verses 52 through 76 are again voiced by the Stoic censor; yet an argument could be posited wherein the sleeper/scribe also speaks verses 52 through 55.[6] This interpretation would require that the "you" of verse 52 (*haut tibi* ...) is not the "you" of verse 56 (*et tibi* ...). Thus the rather sarcastic description of the *Poikile Stoa* (*sapiens bracatis inlita Medis/porticus*, 53-4, periphrasis for Stoic philosophy in general) would (appropriately) be attributable to the sleeper/scribe rather than to the Stoic censor.

Curiously (since we expect the persona of the Stoic censor to be further developed by P.), the primary vehicle of this *suasoria* for a philosophically sound lifestyle is

---

[5] Cf. for the (Persian) motif of "shaping" one's character J. 7.237-40.

[6] Indeed, *Satire* 3 as experiment with voice (and its directive) has generally perplexed critics. Cf. e.g. Ramage (1979) 137 re. ambiguity between second person singular and plural:
> There is at least one instance in which the satirist promotes this ambiguity by shifting suddenly from the second person singular to the plural and back again. This happens in the third satire (63-76), where the recipient begins as a singular ... and in the same line becomes a plural. ... This intentional mixing of singular and plural seems intended to generalize the recipient [of the satirist's advice] still further. Not only is he unnamed and vague, then, but he is even singular or plural.

We must, however, view P.'s "ambiguity" in voice as experimentally purposeful, not merely as a stylistic aid to broaden his addressee (so Ramage, who terms second person address naturally vague): "... the satirist simply takes full advantage of the natural vagueness of the second personal verb or pronoun when it is not related to a subject or antecedent."

abruptly abandoned. At verse 77 comes the introduction of a persona who is likewise antithetical--his words are self-defacing, the contrast between his complete lack of understanding of philosophy highlighting the views just set forth:

> hic aliquis de gente hircosa centurionum
> dicat: "quod sapio satis est mihi." (3.77-8)

And the "populace" is made to side with self-assured ignorance, along with the sympathetic *torosa iuventus*, 86. Thus the function of the Stoic philosopher's persona is now twofold: to stand in opposition (contrast) to ignorance and simultaneously to introduce exempla thereof.

The next voice appears without preliminary introduction:

> "inspice, nescio quid trepidat mihi pectus et aegris
> faucibus exsuperat gravis halitus, inspice sodes." (3.88-9)

This exemplum/persona is like the Natta of verse 31; he is a "lost cause" (cf. of Natta, *demersus summa rursus non bullit in unda*, 34). Even ordered to rest (*iussus requiescere*, 90), demise imminent, this example (of immorality, immoderation) slips into vice self-confidently, affording P. the opportunity to present a curiously vivid account of death (vv. 98-106).

As readers we might expect P. to allow this exemplum to suffice. Instead, in another abrupt break from narrative to direct discourse, another self-confident voice raises itself in protest. The difference here between this persona and that of the indulgent invalid above is simply that this one displays no apparent (external) symptom of disease:

> "tange, miser, venas et pone in pectore dextram;
> nil calet hic. summosque pedes attinge manusque;
> non frigent." (3.107-09)

That the voice here calls his addressee (again the Stoic philosopher) "wretch" (*miser*) underlines not only his self-assuredness, but also his benightedness.[7] We may say too

---

[7] In agreement with Harvey (1981) 103 I do not see compositional or dramatic inconsistency in this passage:"Nisbet, 'Persius', 57, believes *miser* refers to the *adversarius* and that P. must be the speaker. But P. would not defeat the purpose of his own allegory (last n.), while *miser* in the mouth of the

that this second exemplum/persona is a refinement of the previous one. Whereas earlier, physical illness was by analogy equated by P. with moral decrepitude, the speaker at 107-09 represents internal disease disguised by the appearance of physical well-being.

The voice which presents verses 109-118 is entirely unsympathetic with the last speaker. Its general message is that its addressee lacks equanimity, despite claims of healthy self-possession. Listed as disarranging (valetudinary) factors is a series of quite programmatic themes: money (*pecunia*, 109), lust (*candida ... puella*, 110), *luxuria* in connection with appetite (the inability to accept *durum holus, populi cribro decussa farina*, 112), and *timor*, 115. This final voice then assumes that his "diagnosis" of the exempla presented is confirmed by its recipients' response; truth angers:

> nunc face supposita fervescit sanguis et ira
> scintillant oculi, dicisque facisque quod ipse
> non sani esse hominis non sanus iuret Orestes. (3.116-18)

Sani ... sanus appropriately works a double effect. The Orestes "mad" (with murderous intent) would deem P.'s last exemplum intemperate, "hot-blooded" beyond even his (perverted) standard of sanity. Yet *sani* and *sanus* likewise recall the images of physical 'health' (rather its lack) as reflective and symptomatic of moral/philosophical disease.[8]

---

adversarius is suitably aggressive." Indeed, the point P. stresses with "*miser*" is that this voice is that of one indignant, defiant in the face of truthful criticism.

[8] Despite absence of parallels for *face supposita* (v.116) as metaphor, to take it so here is appropriate. Harvey 104 cites one similar metaphorical usage: "For the figurative *face*, which on a literal level denotes the arguments immediately preceding, cf. Lucr. iii. 303 *irai fax*."

2. *Haec Crede Magistrum Dicere:* Socrates As Satirist

It is quite clear from the outset of P.4 that its author intended it to be regarded as a kind of satirical dialogue between Socrates and Alcibiades.[9] What these voices represent is, however, more akin to the representative exempla presented in P.3, for example, than to any historical circumstance. P. makes his dramatic setting clear immediately; we at once know that a Socratic persona will question an aspiring politician:

"Rem populi tractas?" (barbatum haec crede magistrum
dicere, sorbitio tollit quem dira cicutae) (4.1-2)[10]

That the drama is designed as an emblematic assimilation (and that the personae reflect its burlesque nature) is confirmed as soon as verse 8, where "Alcibiades" is imagined as addressing not Athenians, but rather *Quirites*.[11]

The basic message (theme) of P.4 is not far different from that of P.3: Alcibiades represents ignorance of philosophy, ethical values, the predisposition to seem rather than to be; Socrates is physician thereof. But we see in P.4 a new experiment with personae; P.'s exempla of the philosophically ill are incorporated, condensed into the persona of a

---

[9] Harvey (1981) 106 et al. note that at least the passage vv. 1-22 "is loosely modeled on, and exhibits reminiscences of, ps.-Plato, *Alc.* i."

[10] P.'s satiric sarcasm is immediately manifest; note the disesteem in Socrates' description as *barbatum magistrum*. Cf. J.'s generic adaptation of the term at 14.12: *barbatos ... mille ... magistros.* Cf. also Connor (1988) 57: "*sorbitio* ('swallowing') makes taking hemlock sound somehow trivial and hints at a less than totally sympathetic attitude to Socrates." Yet despite this apparent disesteem for Socrates, P. nevertheless develops his cynical character early. *"Rem populi tractas?",* 1, are the words of a cynical wit. Harvey (1981) 106 overlooks the tenor of this phrase, but Lee and Barr (1987) do well both in translating and annotating: "Handling the people's business?" (35) and, "With *tractas* it may well create a double entendre in keeping with the homosexual motifs of this Satire" (118). Thus "Alcibiades" is instantly impugned by "Socrates" as an immoral politician who at once "manipulates the concern of the public" and "strokes the *thing* of the *populus.*" Also of note is J.'s description of Socrates as *senex* (13.185, probably inspired by P.); but J. does not seem to disesteem Socrates at all, presenting him rather as a model of philosophical amnesty (tolerance).

[11] Harvey (1981) 108 notes: "*Quirites*: The form of address is humorously incongruous in a Greek setting." Lee and Barr (1987) 120 repeat: "... humorously incongruous in this Athenian setting." But its function (besides humorous incongruity) is really of course to bring the "Greek setting" into a (relevant) Roman (Neronian) context.

political figure well-known to every Neronian. His Stoic doctor becomes historical symbol of provocative interrogation, mental autopsy.

By this mechanism (historical figure as satiric persona) P. achieves multiple effect. First, there is humorous parody of the Platonic historical/literary tradition. Second, the language of the satire (e.g., its obscenity) is clearly that of fictional voices; thus it may be self-parodic, insulting, violent beyond what is normal for P. *propria persona*. Third, by placing the drama in an early historical context, P. makes it remote from Neronian society, at least ostensibly. Thus the attacks, both implicit as well as explicit, on those (politicians) who seem but are not, are likewise disassociated from the Neronian political ambience.[12]

This Socratic-satiric persona we may also see as an experiment by P. Traditional formalities of Roman satire have been experimentally incorporated within a distinctly separate literary genre--that of the Platonic dialogue. And P. realizes his experiment by introducing into the Platonic (Socratic) context certain essentially Roman constituents.[13] Verses 3-8 are of course unqualified sarcasm:

> "quo fretus? dic hoc, magni pupille Pericli.
> scilicet ingenium et rerum prudentia velox
> ante pilos venit, dicenda tacendave calles.
> ergo ubi commota fervet plebecula bile,
> fert animus calidae fecisse silentia turbae
> maiestate manus. quid deinde loquere? (4.3-8)

---

[12] The reason for this disassociation naturally is to avoid direct, or at least apparent, criticism of the Neronian political structure.

[13] Comm. generally avoid attempts to explain P.'s 'Romanization' of what is ostensibly a Greek model (this is what I termed an "emblematic assimilation," p. 45). Yet Connor (1988) 59 does better: "We should note, as others have, that during Socrates' speech a number of elements are palpably Roman: *Quirites* ('citizens', 8), for example, and *verna* ('home-born slave', 22), and several phrases, like *uncta patella* ('with sumptuous dish'), *cuticula sole summa ... pelle decorus* ('with your skin constantly pampered by the sun'), and the image of the scales (lines 10-13), are deeply embedded in the Roman satiric spirit." Indeed P.'s experiment is not only confirmed by this technique, but also its success depends upon it; for Socrates to seem a Roman satirist (even in part), he must be made to conform somewhat to the prototype (his words must therefore adapt his historical image to his satiric role). P.'s dialogic structure, however, had precedent; Horace's satiric dialogue may ultimately have been inspired by the Platonic format (cf. e.g., *Serm.* 2.1, 3, 4, 5, 7, 8).

Pupille, 3, stands in direct contrast to *magni ... Pericli*, and is thereby accented (cf. also *maiestate manus*, 8, which is ridiculously incongruous in light of *pupille*). *Plebecula*, 6, not only looks forward to *popello*, 15, but typifies the contemptuous language of the (Persian) satirist.[14] Probably the most recognizable occurrence of *fert animus*, 7, is at Ovid, *Met.* 1.1,[15] an instance which would surely be recognized by P.'s audience as exemplary of Roman poetry. We may suggest therefore that P. is here too reinforcing Socrates' persona as that of a Roman poet.

Sarcastic irony continues through verse 13:[16]

"Quirites,
hoc puto non iustum est, illud male, rectius illud."[17]
scis etenim iustum gemina suspendere lance
ancipitis librae, rectum discernis ubi inter
curva subit vel cum fallit pede regula varo,
et potis es nigrum vitio praefigere theta. (4.8-13)

This passage of course implies the opposite of what it actually says (Alcibiades cannot really distinguish right from wrong, even in a capital case). Its purpose therefore is twofold: Socrates' ironic persona is further developed, and an opportunity is created for the shift in manner of address which begins at verse 14 (at which point Socrates will cease from irony to adopt a more directly invective tone):[18]

quin tu igitur summa nequiquam pelle decorus

---

[14] Cf. P. 6.50-1: *popello/largior*.

[15] Harvey (1981) 107 cites this as well as *A.A.* 3.467; Lucan 1.67; Suet. *Otho* 6.1. While a parallel with Lucan 1.67 would provide a socially relevant and politically charged allusion to P.'s passage, biographical evidence precludes us from considering it positively earlier than P.3.

[16] In agreement with Harvey (1981) 108, I assume that Socrates now provides words for Alcibiades, as is clearly the case later at v. 20.

[17] Harvey (1981) 108 cites Hor. *Serm.* 2.5.32 as a parallel for P.'s *puta*, and suggests a translation, "for instance, say." (so too Bo [1969] 72). Lee and Barr (1987) correct the apparent inconsistency caused by the singular imperative, *puta* in combination with the plural, *Quirites*, by taking *puta* out of inverted commas. But equally plausible (according to Clausen's apparatus) would be to print *puto*, and this in fact seems the better reading.

[18] Cf. Harvey (1981) 110 re. v. 14: "*igitur* shows that the apparent compliments preceding were ironically bestowed."

> ante diem blando caudam iactare popello
> desinis, Anticyras melior sorbere meracas?
> quae tibi summa bona est? uncta vixisse patella
> semper et adsiduo curata cuticula sole?
> expecta, haut aliud respondeat haec anus. i nunc,
> "Dinomaches ego sum" suffla, "sum candidus." esto,
> dum ne deterius sapiat pannucia Baucis,
> cum bene discincto cantaverit ocima vernae.' (4.14-22)

In this direct incursion against Alcibiades, the satirist Socrates continues to define himself as cynic, able to distinguish pretence from actuality. *Ante diem*, 15, naturally stresses Alcibiades' immaturity;[19] *Anticyras ... sorbere meracas*, 16, his 'insanity' (lack of philosophical consciousness). The expression *caudam iactare*, 15, while perhaps intended by P. to complement an implied animal metaphor (provided by *pelle decorus*, 14),[20] conveniently too resumes the sexual metaphor begun at verse 1.[21] To dine sumptuously (*uncta ... patella*, 17, "with greased platter") and to sun oneself continually (*adsiduo curata cuticula sole*, 18) are of course the ultimate goals (*summa bona*, 17) of one lacking philosophically sound values.[22] That an old woman (*haec anus*, 19) would be the intellectual equal of Alcibiades looks forward to P. 5.92, where a Stoic satirist (cf. Socrates) will relieve a "patient" of "old grannies": *dum veteres avias tibi de pulmone revello*. That Socrates imagines that Alcibiades will 'inflate' himself (*suffla*, 20) as beautiful and of noble birth again alludes to a standard theme of Roman satire (cf. e.g., J. 8: *stemmata quid faciunt ...*): true merit versus assumed superiority.

---

[19] Comm. (e.g., Harvey [1981] 112) view *ante diem* simply as "before your time." Yet v. 15 seems to recall *Alc.* 1.118B (a fact which seems to have escaped comm.): διὸ καὶ ἅττεις ἄρα πρὸς τὰ πολιτικὰ πρὶν παιδευθῆναι. Thus *ante diem* corresponds to πρὶν παιδευθῆναι, the Greek verb appropriate to (philosophical) education.

[20] Cf. Harvey (1981) 110: "The allusion is to the fable of the ass in the lion's skin."

[21] Thus Alcibiades metaphorically "brandishes" his *penem* at the "seductive" (*blando*) public. Cf. for *cauda, sensu obsceno*, Hor. Serm. 1.2.45-6: *... testis caudamque salacem/demeteret ferro.*

[22] Sumptuous dining, excessive eating, etc. are themes not only ubiquitous in other of P.'s satires, but also in J. especially. For the satiric motif of sunning oneself, see Harvey (1981) 111: "The idea ... is confined to satire." Cf. also J. 2.104-5 of the (pathic) Otho: *nimirum summi ducis est occidere Galbam/et curare cutem.*

Beginning with verse 23, the Socratic-satiric persona embarks on an illustrative confirmation of his theme. Alcibiades as exemplum is spared further self-condemnation (by the words attributed to him by Socrates).[23] Verses 23-4 do indeed relate to the Socrates/Alcibiades 'dialogue' preceding, although the narrative voice of the persona is more generally philosophical:[24]

> ut nemo in sese temptat descendere, nemo,
> sed praecedenti spectatur mantica tergo! (4.23-4)

Alcibiades has been exposed as one unable "to go down into himself," and the idea of seeing only another's faults follows logically.[25] Two distinct exempla follow (the first, vv. 25-32; the second, vv. 33-41):

> quaesiveris 'nostin Vettidi praedia?' 'cuius?'
> 'dives arat Curibus quantum non miluus errat.'
> 'hunc ais, hunc dis iratis genioque sinistro,
> qui, quandoque iugum pertusa ad compita figit,
> seriolae veterem metuens deradere limum
> ingemit "hoc bene sit" tunicatum cum sale mordens
> cepe et farratam pueris plaudentibus ollam

---

[23] Yet some comm. see a narrative shift beginning at v. 23, in which the satirist Socrates gives way to a new persona (that of P. himself). But this is to underestimate the experimental impact of the satire, to oversimplify the poet's intent in an (unnecessary) attempt to attribute to the work a structure which is plain and uncomplex. Of course one might easily identify a shift in narrative style at v. 23, but this need not divorce the narrative of vv. 23ff. from what precedes (and call therefore for a shift in persona). Rather, Socrates, who has clearly been designed as correlative to a Roman satirist, now follows the pattern of satiric personae in general: his theme has been introduced, and from vv. 23ff. he provides further exempla to strengthen it by illustration. I disagree with Lee and Barr (1987) 118: "At v. 23 Persius takes up the theme *in propria persona* and proceeds to broaden out the Satire into an admonition of more general application." But what precedes v. 23 is absolutely of general application. Further, what P. has done in *Satire 4* is to *combine* voices in such a way so as to *equate* Socrates with his satiric persona.

[24] This fact again, however, need not dictate a shift in the satiric persona. Comm. invariably try to account for the narrative break in absolute terms, certainly a mistake given P.'s wayward style of composition. Cf. Lee and Barr (1987) 124: "It seems simplest and most satisfactory to assume that P. now drops the framework of the Socratic dialogue ... Jenkinson (1973) 528 argues that the original dialogue continues, giving vv. 23-32 to Alcibiades." In this case, however, a "satisfactory" reading of the satire need not require simplicity. Likewise, P. is deliberately ambivalent about attribution of verses to 'speakers;' as we have already seen, sudden and dissevered discourse is a wonted Persian compositional trait. Yet Socrates as satirist is confirmed by the allusion, suggested by v. 23, to the Delphic maxim "Know thyself."

[25] Harvey (1981) 113 is off the mark when he says, "The latter idea has no connexion with Alcibiades ...".

> pannosam faecem morientis sorbet aceti?' (4.25-32)

This passage *per se* reveals little, if anything, about the persona already established. Its purpose, besides its exemplary/illustrative function, is to provide an appropriate transition to the next exemplum, which does involve further definition of the persona. The primary speaker of verses 25-32 (who actually speaks second) has attacked (the miserly) Vettidius with the result that he, apparently, will be attacked in turn by another voice, which recalls clearly the Socratic persona of verses 1-23 in at least one place (cf. with v. 18 v. 33):

> at si unctus cesses et figas in cute solem.

And the scenario of one lying (nude) in the sun provides P. the opportunity for a satiric attack replete with delightful obscenity:

> est prope te ignotus cubito qui tangat et acre
> despuat: 'hi mores! penemque arcanaque lumbi
> runcantem populo marcentis pandere bulbos[26]
> tum, cum maxillis balanatum gausape pectas,
> inguinibus quare detonsus gurgulio extat?
> quinque palaestritae licet haec plantaria vellant
> elixasque nates labefactent forcipe adunca,
> non tamen ista filix ullo mansuescit aratro.' (4.34-41)

This engaging onslaught, while ostensibly voiced by an unknown (*ignotus*, 34), nevertheless recalls the image of the "Alcibiades" who might display himself while sunning. While we cannot attribute these lines with certainty to the Socratic persona, we can be sure that the persona is intended by P. to imagine these lines for the *ignotus*, just as he imagined lines for Alcibiades earlier. Yet P. may have intended the passage to refer back to the Socrates/Alcibiades passage in a more direct way. The apparent setting (that of a palaestra) is originally Greek (cf. παλαίστρα). So too is *gausape*, 37 (an odd word for 'beard;' although the origin of the word is evidently obscure, the Greek parallel is γαυσάπης, cf. Harvey 119).

---

[26] Lee and Barr's printing of *bulbos* (although not supported by the MSS) is clearly more attractive than Clausen's *vulvas*. See Lee and Barr (1981) ad loc. for reasons.

Verses 42-52 essentially comprise a summary of the precepts set forth earlier by exempla and illustration. This last section of P.4 is not unrelated to the first (vv. 1-23), but rather serves as a kind of moral. The Alcibiades-exemplum served well to illustrate the tendency to appear to be what one is not. The Socratic persona has shown that, while one may be able to fool others, he must nevertheless eventually admit to his own shortcomings; the praise of others is irrelevant:

>   ilia subter
> caecum vulnus habes, sed lato balteus auro
> praetegit. ut mavis, da verba et decipe nervos,
> si potes. 'egregium cum me vicinia dicat,
> non credam?' viso si palles, inprobe, nummo,
> si facis in penem quidquid tibi venit, amarum
> si puteal multa cautus vibice flagellas,
> nequiquam populo bibulas donaveris aures. (4.43-50)

Here the persona is both philosophical and moralizing. Verses 48 and 50 especially recall the Socratic persona's attack on Alcibiades. The idea that Alcibiades would offer his *penem* to the receptive crowd, that he would in turn *tractare populi rem*, finds summation in, *si facis in penem quidquid tibi venit*, 48. Lust for fulfillment and praise is nevertheless inefficacious (*nequiquam*, 50).

Verses 51-2 finally present the satire's *suasoria*:

> respue quod non es; tollat sua munera cerdo.
> tecum habita, noris quam sit tibi curta supellex.[27]

Thus the Socratic persona of verses 1-23, now as P., has come full circle, so to speak. The admonition first presented to Alcibiades ("Be rather than seem.") is here rephrased in absolute terms.

---

[27] In agreement with Harvey (1981) ad loc., I print a comma in line 52 rather than Clausen's colon.

3. *Vatibus Hic Mos Est*: Anamnesis of *Satire* 1[28]

P.5 begins with a voice similar in expression to that of P.1. There is an immediate protest against (massive) poetic production. The voice which takes over at verse 5 serves P. as *saturarum purgatio*--further justification not to write anything aside from satire. In this satire P. is creating an opportunity to link his satiric program with his Stoic resolve, the appreciative address to Cornutus supplying a spring-board for further attack on those who lack philosophical understanding.

As has been pointed out,[29] P.'s attention to Cornutus illustrates two essential features of satire as Horatian genre: First, some autobiographical detail is provided by the satirist. Second, the figure of the satirist's mentor/father is introduced. Yet another notable feature of verses 1-64 (including the encomium to Cornutus) is that they disclose to the reader that there will occur an evolutionary transposition of the satirist's persona. We will see that in P.5 Cornutus becomes P. And, vice versa, P. becomes Cornutus.

Verses 1-4, in recollection of the literary-critical theme of the *Prologue* and *Satire* 1, serve only to introduce Cornutus as censor. The traditional convention of calling for multiple voices in undertaking poetry and tragedy is introduced only to be denounced (note also once more P.'s use of *vates* as term of abuse and the deliberate repetition and placement of *centum* which stresses assumed enormity of importance):

> Vatibus hic mos est, centum sibi poscere voces,
> centum ora et linguas optare in carmina centum,
> fabula seu maesto ponatur hianda tragoedo,
> volnera seu Parthi ducentis ab inguine ferrum. (5.1-4)

What follows (voiced by the persona of Cornutus) is remarkably reminiscent of P.'s prologue, even to the detail of Helicon scorned. Notice also the recollective connotations

---

[28] At once P.5 recalls the literary-critical nature of the *Prologue, Satire 1*. Cf. Harvey (1981) 127 re. v. 7: "*nebulas Helicone legunto*: For the motif of the poet on Helicon, see *Prol.* 2-3n."

[29] By e.g., Lee and Barr (1987) 135. For autobiography in Horace, cf. e.g., *Serm.* 2.1.34: *Sequor hunc, Lucanus an Apulus, anceps*. For mention of his father as tutor, cf. *Serm.* 1.4.105: *insuevit pater optimus hoc me*; *Serm.* 1.6.89 (cited by Lee and Barr).

provided by *anhelanti*, 10 (cf. *grande aliquid ... anhelet*, 1.14); *clauso murmure raucus*, 11 (cf. *balba de nare locutus*, 1.33); *cornicaris*, 12 (cf. *corvos poetas, Prol.* 13); *pallentis radere mores*, 15 (cf. *pallidamque Pirenen, Prol.* 4). Cornutus essentially embodies the persona of the P. of the program. The praise which Cornutus offers P. here amounts to a summary of the satirist's programmatic declaration:

>'quorsum haec? aut quantas robusti carminis offas 5
>ingeris, ut par sit centeno gutture niti?
>grande locuturi nebulas Helicone legunto,
>si quibus aut Procnes aut si quibus olla Thyestae
>fervebit saepe insulso cenanda Glyconi.
>tu neque anhelanti, coquitur dum massa camino, 10
>folle premis ventos nec clauso murmure raucus
>nescio quid tecum grave cornicaris inepte
>nec scloppo tumidas intendis rumpere buccas.
>verba togae sequeris iunctura callidus acri,
>ore teres modico, pallentis radere mores 15
>doctus et ingenuo culpam defigere ludo. (5.5-16)

At 5.21 we see that Cornutus and P. form a confidential liaison; theirs is a "secret" shared by them alone (*secrete loquimur* recalls 1.119: *me muttire nefas? nec clam? nec cum scrobe? nusquam?*). Cornutus also aids in the Persian self-definition as put forth first in the *Prologue*. Whereas P. compared himself in *Satire* 1 to a Horace who "touched every vice" (*omne ... vitium ... tangit*, 1.116-17), who "jests" (*ludit*, 1.117), who is *callidus*, 1.118, and who is *vafer*, 1.116, and to a Lucilius who could "cut" and "break" in censoring instances of vice (*secuit Lucilius*, 1.114; *fregit in illis*, 1.115), P. is now similarly described by Cornutus--he is *iunctura callidus acri*, 14; he "lacerates" (*pallentis radere mores*, 15); he is *doctus*, 16; he uses jest (*ludo*, 16); and he marks guilt to be struck down (*culpam defigere*, 16). And it is quite clear that the figure of Cornutus approves of these qualities and techniques; he even insists that P. "take what he says thence":

>hinc trahe quae dicis mensasque relinque Mycenis
>cum capite et pedibus plebeiaque prandia noris. (5.17-18)

Thus Cornutus verifies the connection between him and P. In what follows (vv. 19-64) P. does the same in respect to Cornutus, with the result that the two become one, in fact bonded by a "sure federation":

> non equidem hoc dubites, amborum foedere certo
> consentire dies et ab uno sidere duci.[30] (5.45-6)

The connection between P. and his mentor having been illustrated, P. adopts the persona of Cornutus as Stoic teacher. This begins at 5.52, where P. propounds on life in general:

>   mille hominum species et rerum discolor usus;
> velle suum cuique est nec voto vivitur uno. (5.52-3)

But P. as persona of Stoic teacher becomes *clearly* identifiable at 5.64, where the "doctor" presumes to advise both young and old:

>   petite hinc, puerique senesque,
>   finem animo certum miserisque viatica canis. (5.64-5)

To facilitate the development of this persona as Stoic didact there are introduced throughout the main body of P.5 (at vv. 66-7; 83-90; 161-74) speaking *exempla* of philosophical ignorance. Speaking personifications of *Avaritia* and *Luxuria* are provided also (to illustrate spiritual enslavement at 132; 142).

Further, verses 85-6 can be taken as self-reflective of P.'s persona: *inquit/Stoicus hic aurem mordaci lotus aceto*. And the didactic aspect of this persona is reinforced consistently throughout the satire through the manifest recollections of the (didactic) *Satire 3*.

---

[30] Critics have (unnecessarily) stressed the horoscopic importance of the passage vv. 45-51. E.g., Harvey (1981) 141 (quoting Housman): "... P. and Cornutus were both born when the sign of Gemini was rising ... when Castor, the other when Pollux ...". But, it can be argued, the "twin" nature of the P./Cornutus relationship is dictated not by astrological coincidence but rather by voluntary convenience; the two are twins in respect to their literary and philosophical perspectives. Further, the fact that P. does not specify whether Libra or Gemini is the operative astrological agent, and that he in fact admits that he does not really know his own (or Cornutus') horoscope (*nescio quod ... astrum*, 51), may allow us to construe this passage as a joke or parody on the astrologers of the period. That the Stoics seemed to have practiced astrology need not make this interpretation implausible.

At 5. 91-2 P. as didactic persona commands his imaginary "pupil" to "learn," to "drop his grimace" (disapproval reflecting ignorance), and to allow "old grannies" (ingrained prejudices) to be "plucked" from his insides. Note especially the forcefully pedagogic *disce*:

> disce, sed ira cadat naso iugosaque sanna,
> dum veteres avias tibi de pulmone revello.[31] (5.91-2)

At 5. 107-08 the pedagogue points out the ignorance of the pupil about life in general. Although the censorship is posed as a question, implied of course is that the addressee is hopelessly unaware:

> quaeque sequenda forent quaeque evitanda vicissim,
> illa prius creta, mox haec carbone notasti? (5.107-08)

Note also at verses 118-20 the instructive language used by the persona, the dogmatic *peccas* implying of course the superiority of the teacher-persona:

> quae dederam supra relego funemque reduco.
> nil tibi concessit ratio; digitum exere, peccas,
> et quid tam parvum est? (5.118-20)

Moreover, the pupil is ill (*in iecore aegro*, 129), whereas the persona is well.

Mane piger stertis, 132, is most likely expressed by P. in deliberate recall of the similar phraseology of *Satire* 3. But here is realized a reversal of the earlier context--in *Satire* 3 P. had adopted the persona of the recalcitrant "snorer;" here he has assumed a persona entirely antithetical. (Cf. 3.3: *stertimus ... despumare Falernum*; 3.58: *stertis adhuc*). Thus we may suggest a manner of 'personal' evolution. P. has 'evolved' out of the pupil, become master, and the encomium to Cornutus actually points to this transition from its very inclusion in the satire. Verse 154 likewise, while sharply didactic, also recalls *Satire* 3: *en quid agis? duplici in diversum scinderis hamo.* (5.154). Compare this

---

[31] Thematically *ira*, 91, is connected with ignorance, although comm. do not note this. Cf. P.3 116ff., where an ignoramus, who has been exposed by the (Stoic) persona, reflects anger: ... *fervescit sanguis et ira/scintillant oculi*.

with the identical phrase at 3.5 (the first words of the Stoic teacher's speech to the recalcitrant P.:*'en quid agis?'*), and note the thematically similar: *est aliquid quo tendis et in quod derigis arcum?*, 3.60.

After the exemplum of Chaerestratus, whose lack of philosophical understanding precludes true freedom (vv. 161-73), the persona of the Stoic teacher finally realizes the doctrine to which his discussion has been leading. *Hic hic quod quaerimus, hic est*, 174, while referring to one's moral, ethical, and spiritual autonomy, also recalls the message presented at 3.66-76 (summed up in 3.72: [*disce*] *et humana qua parte locatus es in re*).

Finally, P. recalls the popular reaction to philosophical advice described first at 3.77ff. (*hic aliquis de gente hircosa centurionum/dicat: quod sapio satis est mihi. ... multumque torosa iuventus/ingeminat*). This is clearly intended by P. to recall the opposition between the views of the Stoic censor of *Satire* 3 and his antithetical representative (embodied by the centurion). Compare:

    dixeris haec inter varicosos centuriones,
    continuo crassum ridet Pulfenius ingens.[32]   (5.189-90)

And the last line of the satire sums up the opposition between philosophy and hopeless ignorance:

    et centum Graecos curto centusse licetur. (5.191)

Thus Cornutus has been fused by P. with the satiric persona of the program; each one having become the other, theirs is a combined attack on the ignorance which ends in a self-assured, sarcastic dismissal of non-philosophers (e.g., that of Pulfenius). And as a result, the amalgamated personae of P.5 finally display a certain smugness. We feel as though we share an inside joke with these personae, a joke strengthened by the derision of a witless simpleton.

---

[32] Bo (1969) 122 notes on Pulfenius: "cuiuspiam asperi militis nomen, rudis et indocti."

Persona in Juvenal

4. Juvenal 15: *Homines Bestiis Inferiores*

We saw in Chapter 1 (pp. 24-5) that among J.'s programmatic themes was that of *inhumanitas*. *Satire* 15 affords J. the opportunity to develop this theme and to crown his programmatic declaration. The real theme of J.15 is not cannibalism. Nor is the satire a one-sided attack on Egyptian culture. Rather, it is a humanistic plea; its theme is man as less than beast.

Certainly the preliminary views expressed by the narrative persona of J.15 are pointedly anti-Egyptian; the definitive adjective, *demens* in the first verse is assigned directly to *Aegyptos*, 2. Further, the narrator from the outset assumes that his audience[33] shares his abhorrence of Egyptians, asking (rhetorically), *Quis nescit, ... qualia demens/Aegyptos portenta colat?*, 1-2. But the qualifications of the narrator and indeed his purpose in relating the events described are not clearly specified by J.[34] As for the cannibalism itself, the historical event can be neither confirmed nor denied.[35]

---

[33] While the satire is ostensibly directed to one Volusius Bithynicus, of whom nothing is known (he could be entirely fictive or, more likely, may be connected with J.'s patron), the intended audience is of course much broader.

[34] At 15.45 is a personal interjection by the narrator, yet its gross significance is debatable. 15.44-46: *horrida sane/Aegyptos, sed luxuria, quantum ipse notavi* can be read either, "... as I myself have noted" or, perhaps more accurately, "... as far as I myself have observed." Short of taking these words as indicative (as some edd. have) of the biographical J.'s exile to Egypt ca. 127 A.D., we can at least state that they serve to impart to the narrator some degree of authority on Egypt and the Egyptians (he speaks from "personal experience").

[35] Some critics now view J.'s cannibal theme as mere device, and assert therefore that the object of the satire is not simply Egypt and/or cannibalism, but rather the self-deprecation of the narrative persona. It is, according to this theory, through his chauvinistic attitude toward Egypt that the persona achieves self-condemnation. (See for such an interpretation McKim [1986] 58-71 and, in support of McKim's suggestions, Anderson [1988] 203-214. McKim 58 even terms the satire "merely another unpleasant document in the history of bigotry."). As for the possible historicity of the satire, Anderson 205 states, "The Egyptians were not cannibals." Yet this generalization is meaningless, since an *instance* of cannibalism can occur in virtually any "non-cannibalistic" society. Better (and more to the point) is Gérard (1976) 386: "la chose [the cannibalistic instance described in J.15] n'est pas impossible, nous n'avons pas les moyens de le verifier."

At any rate, the markedly sudden introduction by the narrator of the cannibalism theme underlines its status as the satire's *ostensible* area of concentration; the Egyptian practice of abstaining from certain foods is sharply contrasted with their willingness to eat humans:

> porrum et caepe nefas violare et frangere morsu
> (o sanctas gentes, quibus haec nascuntur in hortis
> numina!), lanatis animalibus abstinet omnis
> mensa, nefas illic fetum iugulare capellae:
> carnibus humanis vesci licet. (15. 9-13)

Verses 2-12 serve as an introduction of Egypt's odd (religious) habitude. Their deities set them in contrast to both Rome and the (Roman) narrative persona; i.e. *crocodilon* (2), *ibin* (3), *effigies sacri ... cercopitheci* (4), *aeluros, piscem* (7), *canem* (8), *porrum et caepe* (9), *lanatis animalibus* (11), *fetum ... capellae* (12), all stand in opposition to *Dianam* (8). Thus from the outset the persona has established his status as both defender of Roman (religious) values and antagonist of Egyptian culture. *Carnibus humanis vesci licet*, 13, is suddenly introduced by the persona (and strongly contrasted by what precedes, *nefas ... iugulare*) with the result that the incredibility of the assertion (and too of the persona) is anticipated. Ulysses' account of the (cannibalistic) Laestrygonians and Cyclopes therefore confirms the theme of cannibalism as unbelievable, yet it will simultaneously confirm the truth of the persona's account: Ulysses may be considered *ut mendax aretalogus*, 16, since he speaks with no substantiation (*solus enim haec Ithacus nullo sub teste canebat*, 26), but this narrator speaks of the present day (*nos miranda quidem sed nuper consule Iunco*, 27; *nostro ... aevo*, 31-2).

Throughout the satire runs the theme of man's inhumanity to his fellow man. Stressed is a call to humanity. Beasts provide contrast. Cannibalistic Egyptians pervert this dichotomy--they represent man as beast (or rather as less than beasts, since these are for them objects of worship). The actual account of the cannibalistic *rixa* (vv. 33-92), despite its peculiar detail, serves to introduce the real (larger) theme of the satire (man as actually inferior to beast). The deplorable result of human brutality is stressed again with the introduction of the Vascones, forced to cannibalism by protracted siege:

> Vascones, ut fama est, alimentis talibus usi
> produxere animas, sed res diversa, sed illic
> fortunae invidia est bellorumque ultima, casus
> extremi, longae dira obsidionis egestas. (15.93-96)

There is great stress here (by the persona) on distinguishing the plight of the Vascones from the conduct of the Egyptian tribes earlier described. *Sed res diversa, sed illic/fortunae invidia*, 97-8, clearly shows that the persona is sympathetic, that he understands circumstance. And indeed this strengthens his attack on the Ombi and Tentyrites--their behavior is indeed inexcusable by circumstance.

Whether or not the Egyptians were (or were thought to be) subject to cannibalism is fortunately irrelevant to an understanding of the persona and message of the satire. They are a mere exemplum--an exemplum of perverse inhumanity. Thus the persona must separate them from larger humanity, otherwise his argument would lose force. And as mere exemplum the Ombi and Tentyrites are irredeemable; the persona therefore suggests no cure or punishment for their inhumanity, but simply equates them to irate beasts driven by appetite only:

> nec poenam sceleri invenies nec digna parabis
> supplicia his populis, in quorum mente pares sunt
> et similes ira atque fames. (15.129-31)

Thus the persona of J.15 is certainly anti-Egyptian, yet at the same time moralistic. In fact, the best indicators of this persona's nature are to be found after verse 130. It is indeed difficult to attribute to these lines any degree of personal self-deprecation or sarcasm:

> mollissima corda

> humano generi dare se natura fatetur,
> quae lacrimas dedit. haec nostri pars optima sensus. (15.131-33)

And, while these lines point up the very absence of human compassion in the Ombi and Tentyrites, they serve as introduction to what is no less than a general moralistic plea for humanity. Further illustrative examples follow:

> plorare ergo iubet causam dicentis amici
> squaloremque rei, pupillum ad iura vocantem
> circumscriptorum, cuius manantia fletu
> ora puellares faciunt incerta capilli. (15.134-37)

Again, the persona displays here no evidence of insincerity. In fact the attack on *circumscriptores* is for J. standard (cf. 10.222-3: *quot circumscripserit Hirrus/pupillos*). The stress here is on man's natural instinct for pity, and the following illustrates this perfectly:

> naturae imperio gemimus, cum funus adultae
> virginis occurrit vel terra clauditur infans
> et minor igne rogi. (15.138-40)

It is by Nature's mandate (*naturae imperio*, 138) that man shows compassion. That J. chose the Ombi and Tentyrites to illustrate the violability of this mandate need not reflect bigotry or chauvinism in the persona. Indeed, for the satire to work, an element of reality must surround it; the persona must be credible. The Egyptian context, therefore, as suggestive of remote culture, yet simultaneously representative of a Roman province, gives the satire relevance, the persona credibility. And the image of a child facing death prematurely is certainly indicative of a compassionate persona.[36]

The persona as moralist continues to draw a distinction between men, beasts, and men as lower than beasts. It is only man, he asserts, who has an innate capacity for sympathy, and this is derived from heaven:

> separat hoc nos

---

[36] The apparent humanity of the persona of J.15 has even caused comm. to remark thereon. Cf. Ferguson (1979) 320-1 re. vv. 138-40: "This tenderness has hardly been allowed to appear before in J."

> a grege mutorum, atque ideo venerabile soli
> sortiti ingenium divinorumque capaces
> atque exercendis pariendisque artibus apti
> sensum a caelesti demissum traximus arce,
> cuius egent prona et terram spectantia. (15.142-47)

From verses 147-58 the persona sounds almost evangelical, speaking of a
"creator" (*conditor*, 148) and describing man's emergence from his primitive state:

>   mundi
> principio indulsit communis conditor illis
> tantum animas, nobis animum quoque, mutuus ut nos
> adfectus petere auxilium et praestare iuberet,
> dispersos trahere in populum, migrare vetusto
> de nemore et proavis habitatas linquere silvas,
> aedificare domos, laribus coniungere nostris
> tectum aliud, tutos vicino limine somnos
> ut conlata daret fiducia. (15.148-55)

Verses 155-58 glance directly back to the episode of cannibalism in Egypt described earlier. The persona thus stresses the Egyptians' status as perverts of the humanistic norm. And at verse 159 the persona shatters his idealistic portrait of mankind with the reintroduction of beasts as superior to its present-day representatives:

> sed iam serpentum maior concordia.

The unnaturality of the Egyptians' cannibalism is emphasized more by the fact that even beasts spare their own kind. Thus, implies the persona, mankind has regressed by at least two stages; his status is now below the level of not only the most vile (*serpentum*, 159), but also of the most vicious of beasts:

>   parcit
> cognatis maculis similis fera. quando leoni
> fortior eripuit vitam leo? quo nemore umquam
> expiravit aper maioris dentibus apri?
> Indica tigris agit rabida cum tigride pacem
> perpetuam, saevis inter se convenit ursis. (15.159-64)

Finally the persona draws a contrast. In the terminal verses of J.15, two representatives of early mankind serve to illustrate modern man's inhumanity: the first craftsmen (*primi ... fabri*, 168) and *Pythagoras*, 173:

> ast homini ferrum letale incude nefanda
> produxisse parum est cum rastra et sarcula tantum
> adsueti coquere et marris ac vomere lassi
> nescierint primi gladios extendere fabri. (15.165-68)

And:

> quid diceret ergo
> vel quo non fugeret, si nunc haec monsta videret
> Pythagoras, cunctis animalibus abstinuit qui
> tamquam homine et ventri indulsit non omne legumen? (15.171-74)

Anthropophagy as literary/rhetorical *topos* had considerable precedent before the publication of J.15 (A.D. 127-30).[37] What J. has done in *Satire* 15 is to use this *topos* as an opportunity to introduce a persona whose primary message is a call for philanthropy. This persona is not meant to be self-parodic, although it is certainly a vehicle of parody (e.g., of the singular habits of Egypt, of Homeric epic, perhaps even of historical tradition). Yet it is as moralistic vehicle that this persona is best defined. And (counter to the view of this satire's most recent critics) the persona does not stress his own or Rome's moral superiority over "lesser breeds without the law." Rather, the essential dichotomy proposed in the satire is more general: contemporary man has lost his humanity, having regressed in fact to the point where he has inverted even Nature's ordinance. The persona is a philanthropic emissary; his intent is to distinguish what man is from what he could be.

---

[37] For the presence of the theme in the Neronian period, cf. Sen. *Thy.*; Petr. *Satyricon* 141. Rankin (1969) 384 envisages "a τόπος which ranges from Herodotean-sophistic points of view ... to the school θέσεις of First Century A.D. Rome." Nevertheless, the *topos* appears as the ostensible subject of a single satire only in J.15.

5. Persona of Juvenal 3 (*Saturarum Auditor/Adiutor: Umbricius*)

Our analysis of the persona of J. 3 will begin with a minor revision of the current standard text (*OCT*, W.V. Clausen), which reads thus:

> ... saturarum ego, ni pudet illas,
> auditor gelidos veniam caligatus in agros. (3.321-22)[38]

For purposes of the discussion of the persona in J. 3 (who from vv. 21-322 is ostensibly equivalent to one Umbricius), it will be argued first that reading *adiutor* at 3.322 instead of *auditor* yields not a "much inferior"[39] sense, but rather a superior one.[40]

Those editors who reject *adiutor* invariably support *auditor* because *adiutor* requires explanation; one word obviously was corrupted into the other during the copying of the MSS, yet it is indeed difficult to tell which.[41] Thus certain critics have tended to overstate their objections to *adiutor*. Duff typifies such critics: "It is hard to see how Umbr. could help the satires except by listening to them."[42] Yet in connection with discussion of the use of persona by J. in this satire, it will be argued that there *are* ways in which Umbricius acts as *adiutor*.

The first way in which Umbricius acts as J.'s (the satire's) "helper" is quite apparent. At 3.21 the first speaker, who has delivered the prologue, introduces the second speaker, Umbricius (*hic tunc Umbricius* ...). Umbricius then proceeds with a monologue until the end of the satire; his speech consists of over 300 uninterrupted

---

[38] Cf. Clausen's apparatus criticus: *auditor PRVF: adiutor* Φ. Φ represents "codices *AFGHKLOTUZ* vel eorum plures." Also, *illas* 321 is here taken in reference to "the satires" of J. in general rather than to Ceres and Diana, to whom J. refers at 3.320; cf. Courtney (1980) 194.

[39] So Ferguson (1979) 156.

[40] The variant *adiutor* is in fact printed by Mayor (1877), Friedländer (1895) et al.

[41] It will be recalled that there are occurrences of *auditor* in J.'s program piece (1.1, 166); but *adiutor* is found nowhere else. Of these two variants, one is wrong at 3.322. Unfortunately the MSS offer no help, so the 'correct' reading can be chosen only on the basis of superior sense. One might argue here also on the basis of the *lectio difficilior*.

[42] Duff (1898) 163.

verses. Indeed, Umbricius composes almost the whole work. His indignant persona is what makes the satire, both figuratively and practically. Thus Umbricius, *indignatio* personified, is *adiutor saturarum* in the sense that it is almost exclusively his words which give the piece its substance.[43] Indeed, as J. declares in his program, *facit indignatio versum, qualemcumque potest* (1.79-80). In *Satire* 3, it is Umbricius *qui facit versum*.

While the above explanation is quite simple, it nevertheless suggests other, more theoretical interpretations of the Umbricius persona and his role as *adiutor*. Friedländer does attempt a justification of his printing *adiutor*.[44] Yet he suggests only that a "baurisch Mitarbeiter," i.e., a rustic colleague, might impart shame to the satires simply by his unrefinement. But another, more imaginative theory might suggest that the word *adiutor* is no less than a meta-literary reference to Umbricius as the second satirist, or alternate persona of J., in which case *ni pudet illas*, 322 can be better explained. This phrase would not then imply the meaning, "... unless I shame the satires by hearing them, or by co-writing them," but rather, "... unless I shame the satires by being a part of them;" i.e., by being present in them as a dramatic "helping" persona with which we as readers would be unsympathetic, even critical.[45]

As regards the self-parodic nature of Umbricius, we should consider the etymological implications of his name. At first glance, "Umbricius" could imply "shady character," "ghost" (shade), or something along this line. And it is unlikely that J. chose this name randomly. There are explanations which have been proposed for the

---

[43] Such was the interpretation of some early edd. e.g., Weidner (1889) 62: "Umbricius, der eben der Dichter den besten Stoff einer Satire gegeben hat, will nicht von Cumae nach Aquinum reisen, um Satiren des Dichters anzuhoren (auditor), sondern um als Geistesverwanderter des Dichters ihm weiteren Stoff zu bieten (adiutor)." But that Weidner perceived Umbricius as J.'s ancillary persona, so to speak, is of course unspecified.

[44] Friedländer (1895) 233.
[45] For the unsympathetic aspects of the Umbricius persona as perceived by critics see e.g., Braund (1988) *passim* and Winkler (1983) 220-29.

"shadiness" of Umbricius,[46] one of the most appealing suggesting shadiness in the sense of metaphorical darkness.[47] Thus the *umbra* root in Umbricius' name may have been intended (by J.) to indicate that this persona is not only vaguely "shady," but also that Umbricius is unenlightened in the sense that his opinions are rather ill-formed and he does not seem to perceive his own ethical faults.

But *umbra* can also mean "shadow" in the sense of "reflection" (a reflection evidently was considered by ancient Romans as a kind of shadow). And it is possible that J. intended to imply that Umbricius is his satiric persona's *reflection* for dramatic purposes. And this interpretation is entirely complementary to the idea that the primary satirist (i.e., the one by whom the prologue is delivered) expresses views which overlap to some extent, or are reflected by, the secondary satirist, or the reflective persona which is called Umbricius.[48] In fact one of the arguments against the notion that Umbricius is being deliberately discredited in the satire is that the ideas put forth in the prologue do indeed overlap with those of Umbricius' speech. But if we assume that the prologue was voiced by J.'s primary satiric persona, which is generally motivated by *indignatio*, it follows that the Umbricius monologue simply depicts the attitudes of a secondary persona or "satirist within a satire"[49] who happens to be likewise indignant; and the fact that Umbricius' speech seems to reflect what is said in the prologue does nothing to dispute

---

[46] Most comm. agree that J.'s Umbricius is not identical with the like-named *haruspex* mentioned by Tacitus, *H* 1.27 and by Pliny *NH* 10.6.19. Ferguson (1979) 156 says only, "He is in one sense shadowy, as his name implies." Highet (1961) 253 however, makes nothing of the name, stating, "The name Umbricius is common enough in inscriptions ..."

[47] So Winkler (1983) 222-23: "The clue to Umbricius' character lies in his name. At first glance it appears to elevate its bearer to the heights of splendid <u>Romanitas</u> in its close resemblance to the name Fabricius ... 'Umbricius' is therefore a speaking name which represents the key to its bearer's personality, that of a benighted fool, literally left in the dark about the complexities of modern life in the city."

[48] The similarity of viewpoint between the prologue (3.1-20) and the Umbricius monologue (3.21-322) is discussed by Fredericks (1973) 62-67.

[49] I borrow this term from Winkler (1983) 221.

the theory that the Umbricius persona is not only self-parodic, but also quite self-subverting.

But, to return to *Satire* 3 itself, the opening line reads:

Quamvis digressu veteris confusus amici ... (3.1)

The implications of this line have not been explored by commentators. The question of J.'s "old friend" has evidently led commentators either to assume that Umbricius represents an actual acquaintance of the author or to ignore the reference as insignificant.[50] And indeed, that J. refers to a *vetus amicus* is quite irrelevant to an appreciation of the Umbricius character. Yet what is "important" and revealing about Umbricius is what he says; his words show him to be remarkably narrow-minded. And it follows then that this Umbricius, who has often been construed as J.'s alter-ego, or who is supposedly in absolute accordance with the satiric persona of J., may actually be even more self-parodic than the personae presented by J. in any of the other satires.[51] The reader's reaction to Umbricius when he calls attention to certain (universal) urban ills may rather be one of sympathetic understanding. And of course the criticisms of Rome expressed by Umbricius are at least partially accurate; no doubt criminals and foreign influences *were* quite evident there, just as there were undoubtedly real risks of fire, ruin, oppression by the wealthy, etc. But if we evaluate closely the attitude expressed by Umbricius we begin to see that it is Umbricius himself (or perhaps people like Umbricius) whom J. satirizes as exempla of urban malignancy.

---

[50] E.g., Courtney (1980) 151: "It is impossible to say, and not important to know, whether this is historically true or Juvenal has invented Umbricius."

[51] Mention might be made here also of Naevolus in J.9. Like Umbricius, Naevolus presents what is ostensibly a patient exposition of his personal sufferings. Yet despite the length and detail of Naevolus' speech, he is still presented by J. as an overly indignant, self-parodying expositor. So too is Umbricius, although his self-parody is more subtle due to the more general nature of the ills which he enumerates. A common link between Naevolus and Umbricius, however, has to do with their resentment of patrons (their labors yield insufficient rewards).

At any rate, any analysis of *Satire* 3 must deal with the prologue. What is the purpose of the prologue? Some critics want to believe that its purpose is simply to set up the (probably fictional) circumstance of the J./Umbricius encounter at the exit from Rome. This would give us as readers a pleasant dramatic setting for the satire: J. listening to his interlocutor's complaints about the city, the bustling scene set apart from the quiet serenity of the countryside by the dripping Porta Capena, and Umbricius' furniture resting piled high upon a single cart. Certainly the prologue serves to introduce what might aptly be termed a "reality factor;" thus the larger body of the satire attains some semblance of credibility.

But what is important about the prologue from a critical standpoint is that it indicates that Umbricius amounts to a satirist within a satire; and this second satirist, or second persona is, like J.'s primary persona, depicted as overwhelmed by *ira* and *indignatio*. In fact some critics have viewed Umbricius as entirely "carried away by *indignatio*."[52] And the evidence cited for this includes at least two things: Firstly, the unusual length of Umbricius' speech can be viewed as a kind of unending tirade-- Umbricius protracts his plaintive discourse until sundown, as would only an insensate boor. Secondly, Umbricius is so enraged that he seems to forget whom he is addressing. Instead of maintaining his dialogue with the primary satirist of the prologue, Umbricius starts addressing the entire Roman populace.[53] This is most notable at 3.60-61:

non possum ferre, Quirites, Graecam Urbem.

Furthermore, the implications behind Umbricius' exodus deserve some consideration. Early in his speech, Umbricius declares that he proposes to settle in the

---

[52] Braund (1988) 12.

[53] The change of addressee in the piece is stressed by Braund (1988) 12. But there may be less significance therein than Braund implies; other instances of this kind of inconsistent (non-audience-specific) discourse occur not only in J. but also in other Roman satirists.

place where Daedalus landed after his escape from the Minoan Labyrinth. In other words, Umbricius sets up for himself as his role model, or as an example for himself, the Greek Daedalus; Umbricius will in fact follow his path directly to Cumae. But then later in the speech, when Umbricius is enumerating his disapprovals of the Greeks, he cites Daedalus as the prototypical *Graeculus esuriens*, 78: the starving little Greek, who will shamelessly pretend ability for all things. Umbricius emphasizes this:

> in caelum iusseris ibit (3.78)

and immediately thereafter he says:

> in summa non Maurus erat neque Sarmata nec Thrax
> qui sumpsit pinnas, mediis sed natus Athenis. (3.79-80)

This again is of course another reference to Daedalus, the declared model for Umbricius; yet Umbricius expresses an envious hatred for Daedalus and the Greeks whom Daedalus exemplifies. What is more, Umbricius presents himself as a true (old-fashioned) Roman, with Roman values and *mores*. Yet he is abandoning his *patria*,[54] as he himself states; he will become as it were a *deserter* of his own home town. He even goes so far as to say:

> non est Romano cuiquam locus hic. (3.119)

Thus Umbricius is a self-proclaimed misrepresentative of Rome; a failure who cannot make his living in his own native precinct. And we may suggest that the point J. is stressing here is that Umbricius and people like him do not even recognize their own share of the blame for the un-Romanization of Rome. By resigning from their rightful status as Roman citizens, these Umbricius-types only make space into which foreigners and other undesirables can easily crowd.

---

[54] Courtney (1980) 160 takes the phrase *cedere patria* as "to go into exile" on analogy with Tacitus *Ann.* 13.47.3, but declines to account for its use here.

Furthermore, Umbricius exemplifies to some extent the displaced and desperate client in the patron/client relationship at Rome.[55] And Umbricius even implies that he might, if he could, resort to being a *captator*; yet he asks:

> quod porro officium, ne nobis blandiar, aut quod
> pauperis hic meritum, si curet nocte togatus
> currere, cum praetor lictorem inpellat et ire
> praecipitem iubeat dudum vigilantibus orbis,
> ne prior Albinam et Modiam collega salutet? (3.126-30)

Thus Umbricius implies that he would, if he could, get money for himself in any way possible.[56] And of course J. attacks the practice of *captatio* explicitly in other satires. But the important point is that although Umbricius is absolutely obsessed with the acquisition of money, he simply does not have what it takes to get any. And J.'s attitude toward the overly self-abasing client is not a sympathetic one in general.[57] In *Satire* 5, for example, J. as interlocutor addresses a certain Trebius, who is being rather poorly treated at a dinner given by a rich patron; and at the end of the satire J. reprimands Trebius:

> ille sapit, qui te sic utitur. omnia ferre
> si potes, et debes. pulsandum vertice raso
> praebebis quandoque caput nec dura timebis
> flagra pati, his epulis et tali dignus amico. (5.170-73)

Thus one must conclude that a reading of *Satire* 3 should take into account the possibility that Umbricius is a character who represents that group of Romans of J.'s day which in itself was somewhat responsible for the maladies in Rome which are enumerated in the satire. The persona of Umbricius is similar to that of J.'s personae in other satires in that he is excessively indignant. But Umbricius is indignant to a fault. Thus while

---

[55] Courtney (1980) 152 observes that Umbricius' "only idea is to hang on to the coat-tails of some wealthy man."

[56] The persona of Umbricius is presented as being "no more honest, only less efficiently dishonest" (Ferguson [1979] 143) than the shrewd foreigners whom he enviously criticizes.

[57] Cf. again Braund (1988) 17-18.

Umbricius is portrayed to some degree in a sympathetic light, his overall presentation in the satire is that of an antipathetic character.

Yet Umbricius is indeed an *adiutor saturarum*. His self-defacing monologue provides as much satirical substance as do the various faults of Rome specified therein; these manifold and much exaggerated urban ills (which indeed are almost universal) are presented to the reader by a persona which is simultaneously satirized.

CHAPTER 3

LINGUISTIC VARIANCE IN PERSIUS AND JUVENAL

1. Introduction: Vocabulary

The meaning of P.5 14-16 (voiced ostensibly by Cornutus) is complex:

"verba togae sequeris iunctura callidus acri,
ore teres modico, pallentis radere mores
doctus et ingenuo culpam defigere ludo."

"The words of the toga" seem to suggest simply common speech, everyday language. But P.'s language generally is neither usual nor "everyday." Again, his diction and compositional style are uniquely experimental, involving even deliberately incongruous combinations and forced collocations. The expression *iunctura callidus acri*, 14, in combination with *verba togae*, seems to create a paradox. *Verba togae* therefore do not involve for P. mere conventionality of expression; for P. they involve in fact the opposite.[1] It is with expectation then that we encounter in P.'s vocabulary words which are unique not only to pre-Persian Latin, but even to that later than the Neronian period. To speak of P.'s vocabulary as a distinct feature of his satire is essential, since P.'s catalytic intent is itself manifested in a catalytic use of words. P.'s vocabulary, like his language (imagery), (satiric) message, and compositional style, is itself *aliquid decoctius* (1.125), reactionary, violent (contemptuous) protest against predominant vocabulary (and life). A single salient aspect of P.'s vocabulary, however, an aspect which merits discussion because it informs about P.'s unique purpose, has to do with his (peculiar) coinages, words which are often no less than inventions aimed directly at linguistic

---

[1] Bramble (1974) 3, in a discussion of the passage P. 5. 14-16 likewise sees the significant implications of *verba togae*. Bramble suggests: "To follow the *verba togae* is to profess realism, an insistence on life in contrast to the irrelevances of epic, tragedy and mythology:". While P.'s is a preference for 'realism' as opposed to the affectations manifested by epic, tragedy, etc., even more important is his (linguistic) breakdown of the formal conventions of traditional poesy. Cf. also Bramble 11: "For when he adopts the *verba togae* he also becomes *iunctura callidus acri*: conjunction will now complicate the simplicity of ordinary words, juxtaposed as they will be in more than ordinary - even violent - combinations."

contravention (just as his contraventional collocations aim to disrupt "conventional" poetic phraseology).

Unconventional vocabulary abounds in P.'s satires, and the question arises: To what purpose(s) does P. coin words and/or present (striking) Graecisms? Detailed investigation provides the only means to an answer. What follows here is a representative selection of noteworthy vocabulary.

1. *Semipaganus* (*Prol.* 6), an unparalleled coinage, was seen to serve P. a programmatic function. In connection with *carmen adfero*, the word betrays its sarcastic import, its odd morphology reflecting P.'s indignity, his desire neither to conform to conventional glossary nor to be included in the class of (contemporary/traditional) *vates*. *Semipaganus* alone serves both purposes.

2. *Praelargus* (1.14), another coinage formed by the unconventional juxtaposition of common prefix with standard *verbum*, serves to reproduce, by its own morphological grossness, the grossness of the *pulmo* emitting an inflated poesy (*grande aliquid*). In short, *praelargus* describes the normally indescribable; no standard glossary can characterize the indefinite dilation of the poesy denounced.[2]

3. *Sardonyche* (1.16) and *plasmate* (1.17), both Graecisms (cf. σαρδόνυξ, πλάσμα), stress, with their foreign phonology, the alien character of the reciter to whom they pertain--a reciter who is in fact alien to the point of perversion, indeed a human misconstruction (miscreant), even broken (*fractus*). Hence too the one *patranti fractus ocello* is further described as "washing" (*conlueris*) his *guttur mobile* with "fluid modulation" (*liquido cum plasmate*), a description which is likewise itself a duplicative semantic, if not linguistic, misconstruction.

---

[2] Cf. *praetrepidum* (*cor*), 2.54, also probably P.'s construction. This adjective also by its odd nature underlines the unsound oddity of the subject's *cor*.

4. *Elegidia* (1.51), at once uniquely Persian[3] and a Graecism, describes contemptuously the paltry compositions of *crudi proceres*, compositions in the same category as an *Ilias ebria veratro*. Thus the word is dismissive (especially when modified by *siqua*), its Greek nature and perhaps its connection with (Petronius') satire in this case serving to belittle further the *crudi proceres*.

5. *Rancidulum* (1.33) describes *quiddam* 'elocuted' by a (path[et]ic) pseudo-poet wrapped in *hyacintha laena*--a *quiddam* so abominable that the 'normal' adjective *rancidus* is too flattering. P.'s experimental diminutives express not only 'smallness,' 'triviality,' but also a durable contempt. The abnormality of what is described makes it unworthy even of accessible vocabulary; diction requires invention. Contempt of conventional poesy (and *mores*) dictates contemptuous mutation of conventional glossary. Compare the unparalleled (in its context) *horridulum* at 1.54 for *horridus*,[4] and the most odd *aqualiculus* (1.57) for "belly" (lit. "little water basin").

6. *Plorabile* (1.34), evidently also a Persian invention, is ingeniously bivalent. What is recited by the poetaster (the same one by whom *rancidulum quiddam* was expressed) is on a sad (tragic or elegiac) theme, yet it is simultaneously "lugubrious" owing to its presentation (*balba de nare locutus*), its unoriginality (*vatum ... siquid*) and (presumably) its irrelevance.

7. 'Greekish' vocabulary serves P. in his condemnation of the poetaster who accuses the simple "*Arma virum*" (1.96) of frothiness. The poetaster's '*decor*' is furnished by such Graecisms as (*Berecyntius*) *Attis* (Ἄττης); *Nerea delphin* (cf. Νηρεύς, δελφίς),[5] 1.93-4.

---

[3] *OLD*, sub *elegidion*, equates the word to *elegidarion* (Petr. 109.8) Both words are in fact diminutive forms of ἐλεγεῖον, and both occur only in these satiric contexts.

[4] That P. refers to the poetaster's *comes* as *horridulum* may reflect on the idea of poor composition. Cf. *OLD* on *horridulus* (4): "(of writings) Rather uncouth, not very polished."

[5] Cf. Harvey (1981) 44: "The Graecisms *Nerea* and *delphin* are repugnant to P." And re. *Berecyntius Attis*: "P. is presumably offended by the sweeping rhythm of the adjective and the two Graecisms."

And 'worse' Graecisms appear as he continues with something *tenerum et laxa cervice legendum*: *Mimalloneis, bombis*, 1.99 (cf. Μιμαλλών, βόμβος); 1.101: *Bassaris, corymbis* (cf. Βασσάρα, κόρυμβος). Thus we can say that Graecisms for P. are used to exemplify a poetic pretense which reveals even emasculation on the part of its creator(s) (*haec fierent si testiculi vena ulla paterni/viveret in nobis?*, 1.103-04).

8. *Sanna* (apparently meaning 'sneer,' cf. σάννας), notably occurs only at P. 1.62, 5.91, and J. 6.306. Since its Greek counterpart is practically unique to Attic Old Comedy,[6] it is perhaps the case that P. uses *sanna* to draw a connection between satire and its (old) comic derivation. It is the '*patricius sanguis*,' 1.61, which will meet the 'sneer from the rear' (*posticae occurite sannae*), just as it is P. (and his sympathizers) for whom Cratinus, Eupolis, Aristophanes (1.123-4) symbolize jeering derision (*hoc ridere meum*, 1.122). The *sanna* at P. 5.91 retains the idea of sneering (angry) derision, but this time it is (ironically) misplaced, symbol of indignity (*sed ira cadat naso rugosaque sanna*). So too is the word used to represent scorn in its only other occurrence (J. 6.306),

---

[6] On σάννας and its cognates, credit the following to J.J. Henderson: "Eust. *Od.* 1669.46 says that σάννας means μῶρος 'as if from some proper name' and that Kratinos (337 Kock = 489 Kassel-Austin) applied it to 'such a man, namely Theodotides' (i.e. Theozotides: *IG* ii² 5.3); cf. also id., *Il.* 777.62, *Od.* 1761.20, Photius 499.21 σάνναν τὸν μῶρον. οὕτως Κρατῖνος. Hipponax 118.1-2 West may or may not use σάννας as a proper name: ὦ Σάνν', ἐπειδὴ ῥῖνα θ⟨εοῖ⟩συλιν φύ]εις, καὶ γαστρὸς οὐ κατακρα[τεῖς (where 'nose' may have its metaphorical sense 'penis'). Rhinthon fr. 23 Kaibel uses a similar word σάννορος (codd. σάννυρος, but cf. *Poxy.* 3329 fr. 1), apparently = μῶρος (Hesych. σ 175). ἐσαννύριζεν (should this be ἐσαννόριζεν?) = ἥκαλλεν ('flatter' or 'wheedle') is listed (source unspecified) by Hesych. (codd. ἐσαθνύρριζεν). Dem. 21.58 calls somebody Σαννίων who ἐστὶ δήπου τις ὁ τοὺς τραγικοὺς χοροὺς διδάσκων. οὗτος ἀστρατείας ἑάλω ...: on this see P.M. Clark, *CR* 69 (1955) 245-6. On the 'expressive gemination' of the word's consonants as characteristic of vulgar speech see Schwyzer, *Gr. Gramm.* 1.315. Note that there was a comic poet named Σαννυρίων, cf. Ar. fr. 149/150 Kock = 156 Kassel-Austin. Eupolis (440 Kock = 471 Kassel-Austin) is credited with a use of σαννίον = penis by Hesych. σ 172 = Phot. 499.16 = *Anecd. Bachmann* 361.22, who explain ἀντὶ τοῦ κέρκιον ('little tail'), παρὰ τὸ τῇ κέρκωι σαίνειν ('wag') τὸ γὰρ αἰδοῖον 'ἔσθ' ὅτε οὐρὰν ἔλεγον. Cf. Hesych. σαννιόπληκτος αἰδοιόπληκτος, Arr. Epikt. 3.22.83 σαννίων = σάννας.
It seems likely that σαννν- words are related to σαίνειν 'wag the tail' and were used metaphorically in connection with tail = penis (Greek and German [*Schwanz*]) and wagging = fawning = passivity/stupidity."
Thus it is tempting, given the apparent evolution of P. and J.'s *sanna* from roots connected with Old Comedy, to suggest that this is what may have led them to use the word, since its obscene/satiric overtones meet their contexts perfectly. Yet to pose a convincing argument for this may not be possible.

mocking scorn indicative of profane irreverence: *i nunc et dubita qua sorbeat aera sanna/Maura, Pudicitiae veterem cum praeterit aram* (6.306-07). We may assume, however, that J. borrowed *sanna* from P., P. having first found it a singularly appropriate means to denote 'angry sneer,' perhaps with connotations otherwise impossible to express.[7]

9. *Nonaria* occurs only at P. 1.133. Whether or not this word is P.'s coinage is impossible to know, yet it deserves mention owing to its singularity. The *petulans nonaria* (be it a 'Nones-girl' or prostitute who appears at the 'ninth hour') is important programmatically. Specifically, it is the motif of 'beard-plucking' which is significant; P.'s program/dismissal of readership involves denial of this (standard) satiric theme (cf. Horace, *Serm.* 1.3.133-4). *Nonaria* is simply therefore a typically Persian variation incorporated into the motif. (There is in fact little distinction to be made between a *meretrix* and a 'slave girl'; these amount to essentially the same thing in this context).

10. *Lallare*, in the expression *iratus mammae lallare recusas*, 3.18, is cited by commentators as uniquely Persian.[8] The collocation of *lallare* with the genitive *mammae* is certainly unorthodox (but exemplary by Persian standards)--a typical *iunctura acris*. Indeed, the onomatopoeic nature of the verb and its definite association with 'baby talk' (cf. *pappare*, 3.17) strengthen the admonitory invective of the passage.

11. *Elargiri*, 3.71 ("almost certainly P.'s coinage, inspired by ... Horatian formations," Harvey [1981] 96), of course stresses the idea of 'losing (money),' of giving out rather than merely 'bestowing.'[9] Thus implied is the idea of proper measure, distinction

---

[7] Cf. *zelotypae* at J. 6.278; Duff (1898) 226: "There is no Latin word which exactly expresses the 'jealousy' of lovers." Cf. also *orexim* at 11.127; Courtney (1980) 317: "So Latin lacked a generally current word of this meaning ..."

[8] Cf. e.g., Bo (1969) 53: "Verbum 'lallare' non reperitur ante P."; Harvey (1981) 83: "The verb *lallo* ... may be P.'s onomatopoeic coinage." See however *OLD* sub *lallo* for the word's possible alternate form *lalo* (Pl. *Poen.* 343).

[9] Scribes evidently, not realizing that P. was stressing here proportionality (measure), corrected the passage by writing (the usual) *largiri* (cf. Clausen's apparatus).

between portion and pile (cf. *metae*, 3.68; *modus*, 3.69), reflecting the general theme of the passage: one is to discover limits, define status thereby (*humana qua parte locatus es in re*, 3.72).[10]

12. *Cuticula* (4.18) denotes daintiness. 'Alcibiades' is presented as one superficial, luxuriant (*uncta vixisse patella*)-- as a false semblance of statesman, he represents mere pageantry. Like P.'s *auricula* (1.22, 59, 108, 121; 2.30), the diminutive *cuticula* reflects upon the (philosophical) insalubrity of its possessor. Physical infirmity (of ears, skin) is for P. indicator of psychic, moral, ethical disease.[11]

13. *Gurgulio* (4.38) is problematic. To take it as a metaphorical extension of 'windpipe' (cf. Lee and Barr [1987], Harvey [1981] ad loc.) is to follow the scholiast's suggestion, based on the perceived connection of *gurgulio* with *gurges*. *OLD* suggests however that *gurgulio* is a variant spelling of *curculio*, and gives the (mis)translation 'corn-weevil.' Bo (1969) 78 approaches a more sound explanation by suggesting that *curculio* properly denotes '*vermiculus*,' and draws the parallel, "apud Graecos δρῖλος qui significat et vermem et penem." Given the predominant horticultural imagery of the passage in which *gurgulio* occurs (vv. 35-41: cf. *rucantem, bulbos*, 36; *plantaria vellant*, 39; *labefactent*, 40; *filix, mansuescit aratro*, 41), that P. would intend *gurgulio* as 'windpipe' seems unlikely. In maintenance of the imagery, however, would be to take *gurgulio* as *curculio*, *curculio* as *vermiculus*, 'little worm' as 'penis'. Further, the subject here presented *is* essentially a plot of earth, sprouting onions, 'bracken,' weeds to be 'plucked.' One would therefore logically expect to encounter sooner a *vermiculus* than a 'windpipe.'

---

[10] Lee and Barr's (1987) citation of Hor. *Serm.* 2.2.104-05 (although unexplained) is appropriate. See here especially the idea of 'measuring out' portion from 'heap': *cur, improbe, carae/non aliquid patriae tanto emeteris acervo?*

[11] Conversely J., in apparent adoption of P.'s coinage, describes his own skin (or so does the narrator) as *cuticula: nostra bibat vernum contracta cuticula solem*, 11.203. J.'s 'shrivelled little skin' bears no Persian semantic overtones.

14. *Cornicaris* (5.12) and *scloppo* (5.13) both occur in a passage which recalls P.'s programmatic attack on contemporary poesy. Both words are singularly Persian (do not recur). The words are negative, contemptuous, ostensibly voiced by Cornutus in appreciation of P. As inventions, *cornicaris* and *scloppo* again aim to describe what is too absurd for standard vocabulary. *Cornicaris* (slightly better rendered by Harvey's 'caw' than by *OLD*'s 'croak out') of course recalls P.'s picture of poor 'bird poets' (cf. especially *corvos poetas*, *Prol*. 13), and the absurd self-indulgence of the described is stressed by the paradox implied in *quid ... grave ... inepte*, 5.12. *Scloppo* recalls the idea of over-inflation (with air) furnished by *anhelanti*, 10; *folle*, *ventos*, 11. The word when voiced is itself a forceful burst of air, impossible to pronounce without 'swollen cheeks' (*tumidas ... buccas*, 13). Thus these experimental words serve P. a double and complementary function: they accent contemporary 'bards" 'crow-sounding, puffy bellowing' and set up the contrast between Cornutus' description of them and that of P. (contrast e.g., the consonantal smoothness of v. 15 with the '*raucus*' v. 13).

15. *Artocreas* (6.50), "a rare borrowing of ἀρτόκρεας that does not recur in literature" (Harvey [1981] 197), implies free food, food of a non-specific kind. The word aids P.'s meaning: the "mob" (*popello*, 50) will greedily devour whatever it can get.

In comparison with that of P., J.'s language is destitute of inventive (experimental) vocabulary.[12] J.'s intent is not to dissolve the conventions of poetry and to imply thereby dissolution of societal values; rather, his is a more directly aligned incursion against societal establishment. We do encounter in J.'s vocabulary, however, pithy Graecisms--Graecisms which, like those of P., are designed to reflect some aspect of their author's provocative purpose. These aspects vary:

---

[12] It appears that J. may have invented no vocabulary at all in fact. Among words which may be considered at least experimental are *epiraedium* and *segnipes* (8.66-67), although the context in which they appear is ordinary: ... *trito ducunt epiraedia collo/segnipedes dignique molam versare nepotes*. Cf. however Ferguson (1979) 130 re. 2.65: "*Stoicidae*: coined by J for these pseudo-Stoics."

1. *Archetypos* (2.7) in its context is sarcastic. The 'original busts of Cleanthes' contrast with *frontis nulla fides*, 2.8. The '*tristes obsceni*,' with their pretense for Greek philosophical learning, would ironically accept only 'archetypes,' originals. While feigning philosophical sophistication and severity (*atrocem animum*, 12), these *peiiores* (19) are paradox (*verbis/Herculis ... clunem agitant*, 19-21). So too J.'s *archetypos* points up a paradox: as symbol of (Greek) philosophy, *archetypos* ... *Cleanthas* represent decorum, virtue; yet the contrast between pretense and reality cannot be veiled (*simulant et ... vivunt*, 3).

2. *Coloephia* (2.53) is, in its context, an ingenious Graecism. Drawing a contrast between women and (pathic) men, Laronia states of women: *luctantur paucae, comedunt coloephia paucae*. J. resorts here to a Graecism to capture an appropriate double entendre, possibly impossible to convey in Latin.[13]

3. Amplification of *indignatio* (in this case that of Umbricius) is effected in the description of the *Graeculus esuriens*, 3.78, by a series of Graecisms (3.76-77). That J. describes these occupations with Greek glossary naturally calls further attention to the imposition of Greek upon Roman:

> grammaticus, rhetor, geometres, pictor, aliptes,
> augur, schoenobates, medicus, magus, omnia novit
> Graeculus esuriens.

Only *pictor, augur,* and *medicus* are non-Greek, yet they too are now 'answered' by Greek. Invasion of Greeks is reflected by J. (Umbricius) with invasive Graecism. Note also at 3.67-68 that even 'your [*Quirine*] rustic' is pretending Greek, this by means of

---

[13] For J.'s *coloephia* cf. Mart. 7.67.12. Ferguson (1979) 130 explains: "the athlete's meat ration, but also slang for the penis ... phallic-shaped rolls." *Coloephion* is also derived from Attic Old Comedy; κωλύφιον, "little leg" would have been understood as bivalent originally; cf. esp. Ar. *Nu.* 1019: κωλῆν μεγάλην.

'run-to-dine jacket (or shoes)' (*trechedipna*, cf. τρεχέδειπνος) and 'Nike-prizes on ceroma-smeared neck' (*cerematico fert niceteria collo*, cf. κηρωματικός, νικητήριον).[14]

4. *Proseucha* (3.296) is a term of contempt in the scenario involving (Roman) ruffian and (assumed) foreigner. Umbricius is accused of being a beggar (*ede ubi consistas*, 296) who frequents a 'synagogue.' Thus the word accents Umbricius' self-reflective satire; whereas his speech is largely a diatribe against foreigners in Rome, he in turn, merely by the strategically placed Graecism *proseucha*, becomes object rather than vehicle of reproach.

5. It is remarkable that where J. uses the Graecisms *chironomon* (5.121) and *chironomos* (6.63)[15] he in both cases modifies the expression with the participle *saltans*: *saltantem spectes et chironomunta volanti/cutello* (5.121-22); *chironomon Ledam molli saltante Bathyllo* (6.63). 'Gesticulation/pantomime' are for J. cause for *indignatio*--*indignatio* corroborated by Graecism--Graecism modified by the preposterous *saltans*.[16]

6. The inventive Greek names of the characters in the "Windstedt fragment" of J.6 reveal ingenious puns, essentially parodic Graecisms. The names are without exception sexually significant metaphors, and have apparent import: *Colocyntha* and *barbata Chelidon* (6.O6) [lit. 'gourd (face)' and 'bearded swallow'] imply *os cunnilingi* and *os fellatoris* respectively. *Euhoplo*,[17] 'well-armed,' is an appropriate name for one from whom

---

[14] For Roman pretense for Greek (wrestling), highlighted by J. with Greek vocabulary, cf. 6.246-47: *endromidas Tyrias et femineum ceroma/quis nescit*.

[15] Attributed (wrongly) by *OLD* to 6.62.

[16] That *chironomon* implies disgust is clearly specified at 5.120-21: ... *ne qua indignatio desit,/saltantem spectes et chironomunta*.

[17] Cf. Clausen (1959) who doubts the word and prints *eupholio*. *OLD* suggests *euphonus* ('sonorous'), which Courtney (1980) ad loc. follows: "... it is best to read *psellus ... euphono*, with reference to the characteristic speech of the sexual invert." Courtney's argument against *Euhoplo* (printed, however, by Ferguson [1979]) is senseless: "... the obscure passage Aristoph. *Ach*. 592 ... fails to provide a good coordinate, since even a pervert may possess sexual vigour (O25)." But εὔοπλος at Ar. *Ach*. 592 does lend support to *Euhoplo* as a sexual name. *Ach*. 592 is no less than a (homo)sexual insult: τί μ' οὐκ ἀπεψώλησας; εὔοπλος γάρ εἶ. Cf. *LSJ* on ἀποψωλέω: *praeputium retrahere alicui*.

distance must be maintained (*longe migrare iubetur*, O8). *Triphallo* (O26), 'thrice-phallused' complements *Euhoplo*. Thus J. presents a scene wherein *cinaedi* share assumed sexual names, hybrid Graecisms which at once provide humorous puns and recall J.'s attack on perverse pretension for things Greek.[18]

---

[18] Among other Graecisms which J. incorporates to attack such pretension are notably: *xerampelinas* [*vestes*] (6.519); *ephemeridas* (6.574); *archimagiri* (9.109); *pytismate* (11.175); *hecatomben* (12.101); *chirographa* (13.137, 16.41), the sarcasm of which is strengthened at 13.137-39 by *gemmaque princeps/sardonychum*. Graecisms which combine attack on pretension with simple 'disgust' (in the object/person described) are: *epimenia* (7.120); *acoenonoetus* (7.218); *acersecomes* (8.128) and *cercopithecus* (15.04, although Egypt is the topic).

1.a. Greek script in Juvenal

In connection with J.'s Graecisms are the three instances in which the manuscripts transmit phrases in Greek script. The first of these is at 6.195:

> quotiens lasciuum intervenit illud
> ζωὴ καὶ ψυχή, modo sub lodice relictis
> uteris in turba. (6.194-96)

This 'ζωὴ καὶ ψυχή' assists J. in his attack against women. The phrase's exotic (foreign) sound is ostensibly provocatively erotic (*digitos habet*, 197). Yet voiced as it is (by an old hag: *quam sextus et octogensimus annus/pulsat*, 192-93; *vetula*, 194), it is ineffectual (*ut tamen omnes/subsidant pinnae*, 197-98; *facies tua conputat annos*, 199).

Actual Greek script aids J. in his irreverent parody of the Homeric line, αὐτὸς γὰρ ἐφέλκεται ἄνδρα σίδηρος (*Od.* 16.294; 19.13). That the line is actually in Greek of course strengthens this parody, and the position of the key word (κίναιδος) at the end of the sentence provides the humorous impact. Humorous contempt for the perverts is facilitated by the contrast implied between them and the epic hero. Homer's presentation of (noble) lust for epic steel is replaced by J. in his picture of Rome with homosexual mania; passion for combat has now yielded to passion for homosexual activity.

J.'s γνῶθι σεαυτόν (11.27) falls under the category of fixed-formula proverbial expression. J.'s intention was to stress the mundane archaism of this early Greek (Delphic) expostulation, yet in so doing he adds a touch of sarcasm.[19] That γνῶθι σεαυτόν was originally supposed to have come from a superhuman source affords J. the opportunity once again to exercise a witticism against foreign (Greek) tradition. The proverb "came down from the sky," *e caelo descendit* (27), hardly a serious or realistic assertion, but rather typically ridiculous.

---

[19] Contrast the view of Courtney (1980) 46: "11.27 is a Greek phrase quoted with respect, a unique exception" [to J.'s usual scorn].

2. Juvenalian versus Persian Diminutive

We have seen that for P. the diminutive noun frequently denotes a contempt beyond what is implied in 'smallness' or even 'triviality' (cf. e.g., pp. 80, 83). P.'s *auricula* denotes critical inability at 1.22: *tun, vetule, auriculis alienis colligas escas...?* At 1.59 the *auriculas* described are actually fingers employed in imitation of ass's ears; again critical inability is implied: *nec manus auriculas imitari mobilis albas.* The *auriculas* at 1.108 are 'tender,' unable to withstand the satirical/literary-critical 'acid-truth' of the honest commentator: *'sed quis opus teneras mordaci radere vero/auriculas?'* Critical inability is explicitly, in fact, a universal fault among P.'s contemporaries, as realized at 1.121: *auriculas asini quis non habet?*. *Auriculas deorum* are even of faulty perception; fools therefore purchase hearings: *aut quidnam est qua tu mercede deorum/emeris auriculas? pulmone et lactibus unctis?* (2.29-30).

J. employs *auricula* only once, and not to imply anyone's defective perception. His *auriculae* belong to a statue: *Corvinum et Galbam auriculis nasoque carentem* (8.05). The affinity of usage by P. and J. of *auricula* is not immediately apparent. Yet one similarity suggests itself: whereas J.'s statue is inanimate, crumbling, so its ears are insensate, in decay.[20] Yet too there is the implication that Ponticus' models of heritage originally possessed *auriculae* and, given the Persian implications of *auriculae* as sign of obtuseness (even of animalistic nescience), J. confirms the 'asininity' of Ponticus' ancestral representatives; these '*stemmata*,' even if living, would be for J. mere concretions.

---

[20] Nose and ears are what give a face shape, define it as such. J.'s Ponticus is therefore presenting as substantiation of lineage faceless concretions, the emptiness of his boasting a heritage reflected by the statues' empty expression.

Ocellus[21] is a word used by P. only once (1.18). its modification by *patranti* yields the odd translation, 'with (sexually) climaxing little eye.' *Patranti* in combination with *fractus* of course calls further attention to the paradox of impotent lecher. (I.e. the 'erotic' *ocello* underlines the apparent contradiction which the *fractus* embodies: enervation in combination with concupisence). In J.'s first use of *ocellus* (6.08) there is sarcasm: *nec tibi, cuius/turbavit nitidos extinctus passer ocellos...* (This sarcasm stems from J.'s retention of the original 'Lesbia' reference; cf. Catul. 3.16-18). Further, J.'s *ocellus* provides contrast, marking the dichotomy between primitive ('chaste') woman and her modern-day counterpart ('Cynthia,' for example, is contrasted with one *saepe horridior glandem ructante marito*, 6.10).

J.'s other two uses of *ocellus* (6.109, 568) involve contempt. The gladiator possesses not an ordinary 'eye,' but rather an (erotic) *ocellus*, since he is desired by, and presumably desirous of, women (*sed gladiator erat. facit hoc illos Hyacinthos*, 6.110). Yet his is an *ocellus* which 'drips disease,' his face deformed:

> praeterea multa in facie deformia, sicut
> attritus galea mediisque in naribus ingens
> gibbus et acre malum semper stillantis ocelli. (6.107-09)

Like the (recent) women of elegy, modern woman has an *ocellus*, a 'tender little orb,' to translate J.'s contemptuous sarcasm. The inconsequentiality of the 'itching corner of the *ocellus* rubbed' complements the absurdity of the astrological neuroses suffered by women:

> si prurit frictus ocelli
> angulus, inspecta genesi collyria poscit.[22]   (6.578-79)

---

[21] Harvey (1981) 22 and Bramble (1974) 77 call *ocello* an "erotic diminutive." In its connection with erotic comedy and elegy, so it is; cf. Pl. *Cas.* 136; *Rud.* 421; Catul. 3.18; 43.2; Prop. 1.1.1; 2.26.13; Ov. *Am.* 2.8.15. P.'s *patranti ocello* is therefore a deliberate combination of the 'erotic' *ocello* with an adjective designed to create a striking collocation.

[22] Note also the derisive force furnished by the Graecism *collyria* (cf. κολλύριον).

Both P. and J. employ the diminutive *pellicula* once, and in each case it is a 'diminutive of scorn.'[23] *Pellicula*, like *pellis*, implies somewhat an animal's hide. So at P. 5.116 the philosophically unsound, although outwardly polished (*fronte politus*), retains his 'little hide,' in fact remaining an (intellectual) animal:

pelliculam veterem retines et fronte politus
astutam vapido servas in pectore volpem. (5.116-17)

'Shrewd/deceitful fox' and 'old (little/limited) hide' are complementary coextensions stemming from the image of the ethically ill as bestial. *Pelliculam* here is therefore a derisive diminutive, its explicit connection with *astutam volpem* serving to strengthen P.'s portrait of animalistic unconsciousness.

J.'s 'gold of pilfered *pellicula*' (1.11) is directly connected to its bestial source (it is the 'little hide' of a ram). The scornful aspect of the word stems of course from its employment to describe a Golden Fleece which in mythological treatments is a *res grandis*. Thus the diminutive aids J. in his general attack on mythological treatises. As has been seen, such treatises are for J. insignificant and paltry; this paltriness is reflected in J.'s choice of words by which to describe their subjects.[24]

Like J.'s *pellicula*, *nutricula* (a word not used by P.) at 7.148 can be aptly termed a 'scornful diminutive.' The point J. makes with *nutricula causidicorum/Africa* (148-49) is not that Africa is an extraordinary locus of rhetorical training, but rather that a *causidicus* ('lawyer') will better find support there or in Gaul than he will in Rome. There is irony; distant Africa litigates, supporting lawyers displaced from the center of the

---

[23] Horace employed the word (*pelliculam curare* 'to coddle oneself' is evidently originally a Horatian expression). Harvey (1981) 159 notes that "*pelliculam veterem retines* recalls the proverb of staying in one's own skin," and cites Hor. *Serm.* 1.6.22; Porph. *ad L*; Mart. 3.16.5-6. Again, Harvey also hints at the animal motif of 'hide/skin:' "The ultimate source of the proverb is the Aesopean fable of the ass dressed in a lion's skin ...".

[24] Note also that J. considers mythology a subject too well known to merit treatment (*nota magis nulli domus est sua quam* ..., 1.7). J. in fact proves this assertion since Jason does not even have to be named (cf. the indefinite *alius*, 1.10).

empire. J.'s diminutive *nutricula* therefore underlines his contempt for 'Africa' as refuge for litigators, a place where they flock 'to set a price on the tongue' (*si placuit mercedem ponere linguae*, 7.149).

3. Archaic Diction in Persius

Both P. and J. make special use of archaic constructions. P.'s most 'egregious' examples of archaic dialect are of course voiced by one or another of his interlocutors, either to display their own "boastful and eclectic 'neoterism',"[25] or to disparage another 'classical' poet (e.g., Vergil). Yet every instance of archaic vocabulary in P. and J. as well cannot be accounted for by a simple logic. It will therefore be informative to isolate and examine, first in P., then in J., words which are clearly intended to emphasize, in whatever aspect, the remoteness of 'out-moded diction' and/or 'neotericism' from 'modern.'

Echoes of Vergil in P.'s verse certainly do not always serve to highlight a contrast between valid 'classicism' and (in P.'s view) the invalid 'neo-classicism' of contemporary poesy. Parody of authors such as Vergil is a satiric *generis postulatio*, indeed met by P.[26] Archaism may frequently assist parody, yet its function is frequently otherwise explicable. An examination of some specific instances of archaic vocabulary in P. will be followed here by a comparative examination of those apparent archaisms in J.

1. *Aerumna* occurs in what is P.'s most conspicuous case of archaic-style composition. *Euge poeta*, 75, itself an archaic phrase,[27] provides preliminary sarcasm for P.'s presentation of two examples of poor 'classical' models: "the veinous book of Accius the Brisaean" and "Pacuvius and [his] warty Antiopa:"

> est nunc Brisaei quem venosus liber Acci,
> sunt quos Pacuviusque et verrucosa moretur
> Antiopa aerumnis cor luctificabile fulta. (1.76-78)

---

[25] See Bramble (1974) 126, where the use of archaism in the passage 1. 92-97 is well evaluated. Bramble goes on (174) to declare that, "When archaisms, e.g. *patranti* 18, are used in the first satire, the effect is contemptuous." But the "contempt" expressed by P. in *Sat.* 1 and elsewhere is of course facilitated by experimental collocation, of which archaism may or may not be a part. Further, *patranti* at 1.18 is not exceptional because it is an archaic word (which it is not), but because of its connection with *ocello*.
[26] Salient adaptations of "Virgilian phraseology and diction" are recognized by Harvey (1981) 29 at 1.42, 73, 96, 2.34, 56, 3.20, 51, 66, 89, 4.4, 26, 40, 41, 44, 5.41, 54, 77, 6.3, 30, 45, 76-7.
[27] *Eug(a)e* suggests Graecism (cf. εὖγε) and reminds of (archaic) Roman comedy especially (cf. Pl. *Aul.* 677; *Mil.* 213; Ter. *An.* 345; *Ad.* 911). Cf. also Harvey (1981) 30: "The Greek *euge* is favoured by archaic comedy, and occurs next in P."

It is verse 78 which displays the "warty" style and diction which might be held as an emulative model by P.'s contemporaries, yet despised by the satirist. While *aerumna* in the sense of "affliction" is as old as Ennius (*Ann.* 55), *luctificabilis* is a unique compound clearly designed to parody archaic constructions.[28]

2. It is because P.'s concentration is on the decline of poetry especially in *Satire* 1 that we find the remarkably parodic (with its archaisms) verse:

Romulidae saturi quid dia poemata narrent. (1.31)

Romulidae, dignified in epic (cf. Lucr. 4.683; Verg. *A.* 8.368), sarcastic "mock epic" in P., gains parodic force with its modification by *saturi* and *inter pocula*, 30. P.'s "sons of Romulus" are bloated and inebriated, as is Rome with its poetic/moral disease. That these Romulids wish to hear what "divine poesy" has to tell (*dia poemata*) is not only ironic, but parodic, owing to the epic origin of the adjective.[29]

3. '*Hic ... veto quisquam faxit oletum,*' 1.112, involves probably two archaic words: *faxit* (old form of prohibitive subjunctive) and *oletum* (found only here and at Paul. *Fest.* p. 203 M.). The expression undoubtedly was intended to recall legal injunctions, perhaps even inscriptions,[30] and therefore emphasizes the pretentious "sanctity" of the "ground" that P. intends to violate with satire (*sacer est locus*, 113). It is "impiety," however,

---

[28] Cf. Harvey (1981) 39: "*Luctificabile*, recorded only here, is in the sonorous archaic mould, and recalls Lucilius' parodic *monstrificabile* at 608 (M.)." *Luctificabilis* is an adjective intended by P. to recall not only Lucilius, but also epic and elegiac formations specifically. Cf. *reparabilis* at 1.102 (in a similar parodic context) and *enarrabilis* at 5.29 (although not in a parodic context, *enarrabilis* exemplifies P.'s penchant for unusual diction, a good example of P.'s relatively non-parodic adoption of Vergilian vocabulary).

[29] *Dius* is archaic, found in Enn., Cato, Lucr. et al. That it suggests *poemata* which are "divinely inspired" (*OLD*) makes us recall the theme of divine inspiration presented in P.'s prologue. P. of course uses it in a highly ironic sense (cf. Bo [1969] 18: "ironice 'egregia, eximia', sim."), for which there is satiric precedent (cf. Lucil. 1316 [M.], Hor. *Serm.* 1.2.32). For *Dius* as Ennian parody, cf. Marx (1905) 421 (1316): "*sententia dia* ex Ennio videtur esse sumptum ab Horatio et ab Lucilio per iocum adhibitum in re humili et vulgari."

[30] Cf. Bo (1969) 33: "huius generis inscriptiones locis sacris collocabantutr summaque impietas habebatur talia monita neglegere." Cf. also Lee and Barr (1979) 84, who cite an inscription (*CIL* iv 813) on *discedo*, 114.

which P. will strive to attain; his satires will expose the corruption masked by false sanctity specifically.

3a. Archaic Diction in Juvenal

Like P.'s admonition against writing satire at 1.112-14 (which leads to his self-justification), J.'s (imaginary) admonition, as we have seen, involves an archaic (proverbial) expression:

> tecum ergo prius voluta
> haec animo ante tubas: galeatum sero duelli
> paenitet.' (1.168-70)

1. Commentators have noticed the archaic *duelli*, but have been perplexed by it.[31] The expression has, however, the same effect as P.'s mock-authoritative *'veto quisquam faxit oletum.'/pinge duos anguis...* Archaic language makes the satirists' *dissuasiones* sound imposing, timeless, proverbial, as though carved in stone (as perhaps they were). Thus the satirist presents a solid and apparently shatterproof bulwark of protocol against which he will direct his iconoclastic fusillade; so his violation of this protocol seems all the more meritorious. We are to imagine the voice of prudence returning from the proverbial past, only to be reassured (by both P. and J.) that the time for masking hypocrisy has expired.

2. *Induperator* is an archaic word used twice by J. (4.29; 10.38), not at all by P. The archaism is sarcastic at 4.29:

> qualis tunc epulas ipsum gluttisse putamus
> induperatorem, cum tot sestertia, partem
> exiguam et modicae sumptam de margine cenae. (4.28-30)

As has been noted by commentators,[32] the vulgar *gluttisse* ("gulp down"), 28, stands in stark parodic contrast to the "dignified" *induperatorem*. Similarly, *induperator* is ironically sarcastic at 10.138:[33]

> ad hoc se
> Romanus Graiusque et barbarus induperator
> erexit, causas discriminis atque laboris
> inde habuit. (10.137-40)

---

[31] Re. *duelli* cf. p.39n.43. Only Duff (1898) 448 realizes that "*duelli* ... perhaps forms part of a proverb."
[32] E.g., Weidner (1889) 66-7; Ferguson (1979) 161. Duff (1898) 167 and Courtney (1980) 206 make the simplistic assertion that J. used *induperator* entirely for metrical reasons (contrast Ferguson: "... he could have used many other phrases").
[33] Contrast again Duff (1898) 337: "the form is not ironical here but required by the metre."

Hoc, 137, stands in reference to such *bellorum exuviae* (133) as make-shift trophies (*tropais*, 133), a corselet, cheek-piece (*lorica, buccula*, 134), a broken yoke (*curtum... iugum*, 135), a ship's ornament and a sad captive (*aplustre, tristis captivus*, 136). These are hardly to be considered prizes "too great for mortal men," yet the irony is that they are: *humanis maiora bonis creduntur* (137). Thus the whole passage (133-40) is ironic, not excepting the specific *induperator*.

3. The "archaism" (Courtney [1980] 496) *cumina* at J. 11.38 is incidental (the word's "archaic" form serves no ulterior purpose). What J. has done, however, is to adopt a Horatian phrase[34] and to combine it with his own expression to accent the contradictory behavior of the spendthrift (note the opposite but parallel expressions *deficiente crumina* and *crescente gula*):

>   quis enim te deficiente crumina
>   et crescente gula manet exitus. (11.38-9)

4. Mention must also be made of the archaic passive infinitives used by P. and J.[35] The first of these is at P. 1.28:

>   at pulchrum est digito monstrari et dicier "hic est".

These words are ostensibly spoken by P.'s interlocutor, but this is not the case in P.'s other use of the old form of the passive infinitive at 3.50:

>   angustae collo non fallier orcae.

J. employs an archaic passive infinitive only once:

>   communi dare signa tuba, defendier isdem
>   turribus. (15.157-58)

While it is true that J.'s passive infinitive may here complement his context (he speaks of early civilization, and *tuba* may be suggestive of epic), such is not the case in either of P.'s usages (although it could be argued that the interlocutor's diction might reveal

---

[34] Cf. Hor. *Epist.* 1.4.11 *non deficiente crumina*.
[35] Cf. Hor. *Serm.* 1.2.35, 78, 104.

affectation). The archaic passive infinitive may, in certain cases, be employed by P., J., and Horace also, merely for metrical smoothness. Note that in each case above, and in the three cases in Horace, the word following the archaic infinitive begins with a vowel (an h at P. 1.28). In all cases except Horace 1.2.78, the passive infinitive completes the fifth foot of the hexameter, introducing the final spondaic foot (with anceps).

4. Imagery, Simile, Metaphor

We have seen that in the satires of P. images of food, fatness, homosexuality and disease prevail. We have seen that for P.'s contemporaries perverse diction is absorbed just as food is ingested--their declamations are metaphorical banquets of unctuous victuals.[36] Images of swelling and excess are perhaps the most common representations which P. and J. share. Swelling is often linked by P. with disease; fatness, insalubrity, moral, ethical, and critical sickness are characteristics of the swollen.

It is the slack student, the one who cannot write ostensibly because of a bad pen, really because of sluggishness, who "explodes, glassy bile swelling within:"

> turgescit vitrea bilis:
> findor, ut Arcadiae pecuaria rudere credas. (P. 3.8-9)

As we have observed, anger (bile) indicates ignorance for P.[37] Imagery of swelling implies fatness and anger at the same time, both in themselves suggestive of ignorant sloth. P. retains the idea suggested by *turgescit*, 8, with the introduction of Natta at 3.31. See here especially the connected themes of fatness, self-indulgence, stupidity and moral perdition:

> non pudet ad morem discincti vivere Nattae.
> sed stupet hic vitio et fibris increvit opimum
> pingue, caret culpa, nescit quid perdat, et alto
> demersus summa rursus non bullit in unda. (3.31-34)

Later in *Satire* 3 P. returns to imagery of swelling, this time in combination with physical, beyond ethical, disease:

> "heus bone, tu palles." "nihil est." "videas tamen istuc,
> quidquid id est. surgit tacite tibi lutea pellis."
> "at tu deterius palles, ne sis mihi tutor.
> iam pridem hunc sepeli; tu restas." "perge, tacebo."
> turgidus hic epulis atque albo ventre lavatur,
> gutture sulpureas lente exhalante mefites. (3.94-99)

---

[36] See Bramble (1974) 50 ff. for a full discussion of the history of "metaphor of literary diet" in both Greek and Roman literature, from Pind. through Quint.
[37] See p.55 n.31.

The ethical disease suffered by the one with "bloated skin" (*surgit ... lutea pellis*, 95) naturally manifests itself eventually in physical disease and finally death (*in portam rigidas calces extendit*, 3.105). Fatness creeps upon him quietly, unperceived (*tacite*, 95). P.'s image of the philosophically lost, while primarily involving the notion of fatness (*surgit ... pellis, turgidus*, 95, 98), is complemented by a suggestion of (bird-like) rapacity (recall once more P.'s *venter* of the *Prologue* and note that *guttur* suggests a bird's crop;[38] cf. *albo ventre, gutture*, 98-99).

P.5 is replete with swelling imagery. There are three salient instances of this, two of them in the introduction to Cornutus (vv. 1-29). P.'s are not "swollen cheeks" (*nec ... tumidas ... buccas*, 5.13), nor will he have his page "swell to lend weight to smoke" (*non ... pagina turgescat dare pondus idonea fumo*, 19-20). Rather, it is in the description of one of P.'s examples of worthless living where "singular vow" (*voto vivitur uno*, 53) is "to swell in well-watered sleep," an occupation in the same category as the spice trade, immersion in games and gambling, or venereal absorbtion:

> mercibus hic Italis mutat sub sole recenti
> rugosum piper et pallentis grana cumini,
> hic satur inriguo mavult turgescere somno,
> hic campo indulget, hunc alea decoquit, ille
> in venerem putris. (5.54-58)

J. comes closest to P.'s imagery of swelling with his images of excess. Gluttony as theme lends J. recurrent opportunity to introduce this excess-imagery. Naturally, these images are developed most notably in *Satires* 4 and 5, where the underlying themes involve (extravagant) dinner-parties.

At 4.28 J. embarks on gluttony as theme, the key words *gluttisse* and *ructarit* (28, 31) introducing imagery of crapulence--imagery which resurfaces throughout the satire:

> qualis tunc epulas ipsum gluttisse putamus
> induperatorem, cum tot sestertia, partem
> exiguam et modicae sumptam de margine cenae,

---

[38] See e.g., *OLD* on *guttur*, which cites, in reference to birds, Col. 8.5.17; Plin. *Nat.* 11.200.

> purpureus magni ructarit scurra Palati,
> iam princeps equitum, magna qui voce solebat
> vendere municipes fracta de merce siluros? (4.28-33)

At J. 5.80ff. the descriptive image of the food served reflects and clarifies the status of lower-class versus privileged:

> aspice quam longo distinguat pectore lancem
> quae fertur domino squilla, et quibus undique saepta
> asparagis qua despiciat convivia cauda,
> dum venit excelsi manibus sublata ministri.
> sed tibi dimidio constrictus cammarus ovo
> ponitur exigua feralis cena patella. (5.80-85)

In short, what J. implies with this description is that the wealthy host seems a "lobster with a long chest," while the inferior guest is a mere "shrimp," closed in (*constrictus*, 84) by half an egg. Thus the passage serves as metaphor for social circumstance. The master of the dinner, like the lobster, metaphorically "looks down upon" (*despiciat*, 82) the guest, whose significance is akin to that of a corpse (his serving is a "funeral offering" [*feralis cena*, 85]).

Another image which P. and J. share involves Lucilius as warrior. Both P. and J. present Lucilius with direct military imagery; P.'s *secuit Lucilius urbem* (1.114) is transferred by J. out of metaphor and brought into simile: *ense velut stricto quotiens Lucilius ardens/infremuit* (1.165-6). Notable in J.'s simile is the use of *infremuit* to describe Lucilius' "war cry," since the word would *per se* conjure up images of Lucilius as raging, even ferocious.[39] J., however, in contrast to P., extends the Lucilius-as-warrior metaphor (simile) to include himself (the satirist). As we have seen, J. presents the metaphor of satirist as warrior in his (interlocutor's) *dissuasio*:

> 'haec animo ante tubas: galeatum sero duelli
> paenitet.' (1.169-70)

---

[39] Cf. e.g., *infremuitque ferox* (*aper*), Verg. A. 10.711; *infremuit leo*, Sil. 11.245.

J.'s description of the youth who neither depilates nor frequents public baths with exposed genitals recalls P.'s metaphorical image of the young (pathic) Alcibiades at 4.35ff. Here is the passage in P.:

> 'hi mores! penemque arcanaque lumbi
> rucantem populo marcentis pandere bulbos.[40]
> tum, cum maxillis balanatum gausape pectas,
> inguinibus quare detonsus gurgulio extat?
> quinque palaestritae licet haec plantaria vellant
> elixasque nates labefactent forcipe adunca,
> non tamen ista filix ullo mansuescit aratro.' (4.35-41)

Here is J.:

> nec pupillares defert in balnea raucus[41]
> testiculos, nec vellendas iam praebuit alas,
> crassa nec opposito pavidus tegit inguina guto. (11.156-58)

P.'s description is actually a metaphor (as has been noted): the pathic youth is a weed-ridden patch of ground. Nevertheless, J.'s image retains at least two Persian sub-themes: depilation, public exhibition of testicles. J. has therefore incorporated an essentially Persian metaphor into his imagistic description of what a youth should not be. J. does, however, in an unrelated passage, incorporate briefly the (Persian) metaphor of pathic as ground (to be plowed or cultivated), this at 2.9-10:

> castigas turpia, cum sis
> inter Socraticos notissima fossa cinaedos?

Fossa, "ditch," is a metaphorical expression which is even more explicit than P.'s "patch of ground," since the implied notion of "being plowed" is indicative of the pathic's passive homosexual role.

P.'s metaphors involving birds as poets have been discussed (Ch. 1), especially in connection with P.'s programmatic prologue. Likewise, we have seen that P. is not to be counted among "bird-like" poets: *nec ... cornicaris inepte*, 5. 11-12. Notably, J. too

---

[40] On *bulbos* vs. *vulvas* cf. p.50n.26.
[41] For *raucus*, Ferguson (1979) argues for, and prints, *draucus*, "sodomite." Yet *raucus*, in the sense of "husky" or "harsh-sounding," craetes a humorous paradox in combination with the diminutive *pupillares ... testiculos* and *pavidus*.

connects certain persons to birds. His first such comparison is a metaphor at 2.63, a verse voiced ostensibly by Laronia:

> 'dat veniam corvis, vexat censura columbas.'

"The (moralistic) censor grants leniency to crows," asserts Laronia, yet "persecutes doves." Indeed, the point of the metaphor hinges on sexuality, the perverse "crows" being ignored, the innocent "doves" being blamed unjustly.[42]

J.'s second comparison of person to bird is at 3.90-91, a simple case illustrating (Greek) insincerity in (musical) criticism:

> miratur vocem angustam, qua deterius nec
> ille sonat quo mordetur gallina marito?

This comparison is straight-forward and uncomplicated, since a more irritating screech than a cock's crow is impossible to imagine.[43]

J.'s final human-as-bird correlation is the simile at 10.230-32, wherein a geriatric is likened to an infant swallow:

> ipse ad conspectum cenae deducere rictum
> suetus hiat tantum ceu pullus hirundinis, ad quem
> ore volat pleno mater ieiuna.

This simile conjures up another of J.'s intentionally grotesque images of the geriatric, the hungry helplessness of the baby swallow accurately reflective of the geriatric's dependence.

J. too presents an image of the generic geriatric as impotent, an image even more common in P. Here is J. 10.204-08:

> nam coitus iam longa oblivio, vel si
> coneris, iacet exiguus cum ramice nervuus

---

[42] The scholiast (ed. Wessner 1967) on 2.63 suggests that crows proverbally symbolized sexual perversion since they were said to have oral intercourse: "proverbium est corvorum de impudicis ... unde dicunt coire corvos per os et sic parere." If this proverb was well-known, perhaps it reflects also somewhat on P.'s "crow-poets." Courtney (1980) 132 sees irony in the crow/dove dichotomy, since "*corvi* ... prey on *columbae*."

[43] However, as Ferguson (1979) 143 notes, "In addition there may be an allusion to the high-pitched tones of the eunuch-priests of Cybele (*galli*), such as Martial makes ...".

> et, quamvis tota palpetur nocte, iacebit.
> anne aliquid sperare potest haec inguinis aegri
> canities?

Here the old man is presented metaphorically as "this white hair of an ill penis," the effect of which is to dehumanize the subject while simultaneously (over)stressing his sexual impotence.

P.'s first image of age similarly stresses decay of sexual ability as reflected by external symptom. "Skin" and "joints," by their deteriorated state, reflect the subject's impotence:

> tun, vetule, auriculis alienis colligas escas,
> articulis quibus et dicas cute perditus 'ohe'? (1.22-23)

There is stress here too on the geriatric's desire (libido), which remains (perversely) undiminished, although physically the old man cannot function; the geriatric therefore is presented as paradoxical.

Likewise for P., Rome itself is, like its contemporary literary representatives, emasculated:

> haec fierent si testiculi vena ulla paterni
> viveret in nobis? summa delumbe saliva
> hoc natat in labris et in udo est Maenas et Attis
> nec pluteum caedit nec demorsos sapit unguis. (1.103-06)

Emasculate verse reflects the image of an emasculate Rome, and the image is complete; not even a vein of paternal testicle remains. Similarly, *nostrum hoc maris expers* (6.39)[44] is blamed for infecting not only the literary and philosophical circles of Rome, but even the common farmer:

> 'tune bona incolumis minuas?' et Bestius urguet
> doctores Graios: ita fit; postquam sapere urbi
> cum pipere et palmis venit nostrum hoc maris expers,
> fenisecae crasso vitiarunt unguine pultes.' (6.37-40)

---

[44] As noted by Harvey (1981) 194, *maris expers* is Horatian (*Serm.* 2.8.15) and works as a pun in Hor. ("emasculate" and "without sea-water") The pun does not work here in P.; yet *sapere* ("taste" and "to be philosophical"), itself ambiguous, receives two possible connotations with *piper et palmis*.

CHAPTER 4

FORM VERSUS MEANING: THE SATIRIC MESSAGE

1. The Philosophical Message in Persius

P. as poet has been described as "never amusing ... always moralistic."[1] That P. reveals his Stoic background is certainly the case,[2] yet his satires do not of course constitute mere philosophical doctrine. Whatever urgency toward philosophy which might be extracted from the satires is more or less incidental to P.'s urgency away from the vices which constitute his programmatic themes: e.g., greed, perversion, pretension, and effeminacy.[3]

P.'s "steam-cleaned ear" is a sign of philosophical receptivity. Ears uncleaned, among other symptoms, mark those lacking in philosophical health and values. This connection between the clean ear and the philosophical is so strong in P. that he hints at it even in his program:

inde vaporata lector mihi ferveat aure. (1.126)

What P. requires is a reader whose ears will receive, or at least be clear to receive, instruction. This is important enough to be stressed here in the program precisely because philosophical instruction will play a large role in P.'s remaining satires.[4] From the outset, then, P. suggests a dichotomy between those who can 'hear' and those who are 'deaf.'

Yet P.'s ear/instruction metaphor gives rise to further metaphor. Not only must one who aspires to philosophical health have clean ears, but he must also allow the

---

[1] Ferguson (1979) xv.
[2] As pointed out by Lee and Barr (1987) 2, P. was an associate of well-known Neronian philosophers (e.g., Cornutus, Thrasea Paetus): "Thrasea was the leader of a group of like-minded individuals sometimes called the 'Stoic opposition', who regulated their conduct by the teachings of that sect and created a centre of conspicuous disapproval of the Neronian regime for which numbers of them eventually suffered."
[3] Indeed, we would expect from a Stoic *doctor* consistent exhortation to adopt *virtus* as the *summum bonum*, yet there is no such thing in P. *Virtus* is in fact mentioned only once in the satires; the exhortation to adopt it is implicit, not explicit: *virtutem videant intabescantque relicta*, 3.38.
[4] *Ferveat*, 126, while supplementing the culinary imagery supplied by *aliquid decoctius*, 125, likewise implies that P. desires only an eager reader, one who metaphorically "burns" for P.'s message.

(proper) "farmer" to "plant" the appropriate "fruit" in these same ears. Thus P. credits Cornutus with "sowing his purged ears with Cleanthean fruit:"

>   cultor enim iuvenum purgatas inseris aures
>   fruge Cleanthea. (5.63-4)

And the blossom of this fruit (Stoicism) directs the disposition and yields "travelling provisions" for old age:

>   petite hinc, puerique senesque,
>   finem animo certum miserisque viatica canis. (5.64-5)

P.'s (philosophical) ear is the metaphorical mind/soul, a fact which becomes clearly evident finally at 5.85-7:

>   "mendose colligis" inquit
>   Stoicus hic aurem mordaci lotus aceto,
>   "hoc relicum accipio, 'licet' illud et 'ut volo' tolle."

Unlike the philosophically misguided, the "Stoic" can distinguish true from imagined freedom, this owing again to an "ear" which, in this case, has been washed with "acidic vinegar." The notion of a caustic solution (vinegar) of course vivifies P.'s ear-imagery, since it is this with which contemporary Romans cleaned their ears in actuality. And this vivification lends an equation, equally vivid yet metaphorical: a scoured ear is free of fat (wax), pollution which prevents aural perception; a scoured mind/soul is likewise free of pollution, and is therefore capable of profound philosophical perception.

The pollution which impedes the philosophically ill from the path to wellness is for P. not a single entity. In *Satire* 5, for example, there are given at least four factors to which the philosophically deprived fall victim: *Avaritia*, the lack of a concept of the divine, *Luxuria*, and *Ambitio*.

Avaritia, asserts P., is to those subject to psychic pollution, one of many internal masters. Although one's natural inclination may be toward leisure and sloth, *Avaritia* holds the power of enslavement:

>   ·mane piger stertis. "surge" inquit Avaritia, "eia

> surge." negas. instat. "surge" inquit. "non queo." "surge."
> "et quid agam?" "rogat! en saperdas advehe Ponto,
> castoreum, stuppas, hebenum, tus, lubrica Coa." (5.132-35)

Greed and divinity are incompatible in P.'s philosophical outlook. Thus if one is slave to *Avaritia*, he must necessarily ignore (the justice of) Juppiter:

> "verte aliquid. iura." [5] "sed Iuppiter audiet." "eheu,
> baro, regustatum digito terebrare salinum
> contentus perages, si vivere cum Iove tendis." [6] (5.137-39)

Yet the voice of *Luxuria*, although antithetical to that of *Avaritia*, is, for one unprotected by philosophy, an equally formidable and influential master. The "philosophical slave" is therefore "torn by a double hook," nor can such a person "break his chain" entirely:[7]

> ocius ad navem! nihil obstat quin trabe vasta
> Aegaeum rapias, ni sollers Luxuria ante
> seductum moneat: "quo deinde, insane, ruis, quo?" (5.141-43)

And the voice of *Luxuria* here shows itself to be precisely at odds with *Avaritia*'s dictates:

> "indulge genio, carpamus dulcia, nostrum est
> quod vivis, cinis et manes et fabula fies,
> vive memor leti, fugit hora, hoc quod loquor inde est." (5.151-53)

P.'s message concentrates on the philosophical cripple's hopelessness. The pollution which infects his psyche is manifold, with the result that even if one aspect thereof is consciously resisted, another aspect nevertheless predominates. Error, therefore, is 'alternating:'

> en quid agis? duplici in diversum scinderis hamo.

---

[5] Edd. disagree on the meaning of *verte aliquid. iura*; Harvey (1981) 164 insists that its only correct meaning is "'borrow some money;' swear you will repay it.' As Jahn notes, *verte* is a typical variation on the technical *versuram fac* (80n.)." Lee and Barr (1987) 150 reply on *verte aliquid*: "'Deal in *something*.'" Given the context of trade which governs 5.132-50, Lee and Barr's interpretation is the more attractive. Yet *verte aliquid*, as well as *iura*, loses nothing by being allowed semantic ambiguity; the expression in fact, by its ambiguity, magnifies the ambiguous and vague call to riches and litigation which *Avaritia* makes.

[6] The imprisonment of the *animus/anima* by *Avaritia* is resumed at 6.75ff. (*vende animam lucro* ...). Cf. Lee and Barr (1987) 167: "The thematic link between the conclusion of the satire and the rest seems to be the heir's greed."

[7] Cf. 5.160 (... *a collo trahitur pars longa catenae*) with 5.118 for P.'s 'leashing' metaphor (... *funemque reduco*).

> huncine an hunc sequeris? subeas alternus oportet
> ancipiti obsequio dominos, alternus oberres. (5.154-56)

Further, the hopeless aspect of the philosophical cripple's life is stressed by P. with a dog-metaphor, the point of which is that only temporary escape from one's 'internal masters' is possible. Philosophical health is, according to P., therefore absolute;[8] philosophical illness is chronic and recurrent:

> nec tu, cum obstiteris semel instantique negaris
> parere imperio, 'rupi iam vincula' dicas;
> nam et luctata nodum abripit, et tamen illi,
> cum fugit, a collo trahitur pars longa catenae. (5.157-60)

Ambitio is presented as the motivating 'master' of the philosophical cripple who is led to pursue politics. As we have seen with Alcibiades in *Satire* 4, P.'s politician is the one most in need of philosophical understanding, yet among the last to accept it (along with the 'tribe of centurions'). Here P. presents *Ambitio* as able to drag a political aspirant so possessed that he "gapes" (implying of course blind stupidity):

> ius habet ille sui Palpo[9] quem ducit hiantem
> cretata Ambitio? "vigila et cicer ingere large
> rixanti populo, nostra ut Floralia possint
> aprici meminisse senes. quid pulcherius?" (5.176-79)

P.'s imagined penalty for the politician may strike the reader as odd, unless we recognize that what P. has been so far stressing is the ability of *Ambitio* to drive from the mind all common sense. Further, the unpredictable nature of popular politics itself may be hinted at with the politician's superstitious suffering:[10]

>   at cum
> Herodis venere dies unctaque fenestra
> dispositae pinguem nebulam vomuere lucernae

---

[8] For the absolute nature of P.'s (Stoic) philosophy, cf. also 5.119-21, the message of which is that even the slightest action of one lacking reason brings "sin:"
> nil tibi concessit ratio; digitum exere, peccas,
> et quid tam parvum est? sed nullo ture litabis,
> haerat in stultis brevis ut semiunca recti.

[9] Lee and Barr's capitalization of Clausen's *palpo* is attractive due to the semantic significance thereby imparted to what is then the name of the political aspirant (cf. *Cerdo*, 4.51, also in Lee and Barr's text).

[10] P. may also include here a deliberate stab at the foreign religion of his day, if "the subject of these lines [is] a Roman convert to Judaism." (Lee and Barr [1987] 154).

> portantes violas rubrumque amplexa catinum
> cauda natat thynni et tumet alba fidelia vino,
> labra moves tacitus recutitaque sabbata palles. (5.180-85)

A good part of P.'s philosophical message involves a call to "Reason" (*ratio*), by which psychic slavery can be avoided. P.'s *ratio* includes not only the vague notion of "understanding," but also retains ideas of proportionality, measure, and calculation[11] (even of one's personal limitations and *locus* in the larger "human thing"). Note in the following passage these components of *ratio*: order (proper placement), limit, measure (proper monetary expenditure), and self-knowledge:

> discite et, o miseri, causas cognoscite rerum:
> quid sumus et quidnam victuri gignimur, ordo
> quis datus, aut metae qua mollis flexus et unde,
> quis modus argento, quid fas optare, quid asper
> utile nummus habet, patriae carisque propinquis
> quantum elargiri deceat, quem te deus esse
> iussit et humana qua parte locatus es in re. (3.66-72)

The admonitions "Be Yourself" and "Know Yourself" (as components of *ratio*) are indeed the final presentations of *Satire* 4. Yet what precludes for most the adoption of these maxims is a general unwillingness to engage in introspection (the inevitable result of which is of course philosophical illness):

> ut nemo in sese temptat descendere, nemo,
> sed praecedenti spectatur mantica tergo! (4.23-4)

Thus it is that P. insists that we "spit out what we are not." This done, introspection adopted, one will realize the shortcomings of his (natural) furnishings:

> respue quod non es; tollat sua munera Cerdo.
> tecum habita: noris quam sit tibi curta supellex. (4.51-2)

When P. speaks of *ratio*, then, in *Satire* 5, we must realize that he is speaking of a compound concept--a concept which, once adopted, is multivalent in the direction of the mind/soul to Stoic *libertas* (*libertate opus est*, 5.73). And for P., Cornutus stands not

---

[11] Note at 5.107-08 especially the idea of rational calculation, here expressed in concrete terms:
> quaeque sequenda forent quaeque evitanda vicissim,
> illa prius creta, mox haec carbone notasti?

only as exemplar of Stoic *libertas*, but also as "Socratic" regulator of *animi* which tend away from *ratio*. Here P. admits his philosophical debt to Cornutus, credits him with "straightening his contorted *mores*," and finally subjecting his mind to *ratio*:

> me tibi supposui, teneros tu suscipis annos
> Socratico, Cornute, sinu. tum fallere sollers
> adposita intortos extendit regula mores
> et premitur ratione animus vincique laborat
> artificemque tuo ducit sub pollice voltum. (5.36-40)

Action, asserts P., is dictated by *ratio*; ignorance (lack of *ratio*) and action in combination, *ratio* therefore forbids. If one lives and acts by rational dictates, he will likewise live in accord with public law and human nature; if not, shame will be the only fruit of action:

> stat contra ratio et secretam gannit in aurem,[12]
> ne liceat facere id quod quis vitiabit agendo.
> publica lex hominum naturaque continet hoc fas,
> ut teneat vetitos inscita debilis actus. (5.96-99)

What then is the *summum bonum* proposed in P.'s satires, his purpose in advocating *ratio*? We may accurately suggest that it is *libertas*, true freedom--a freedom of the *animus* which can be realized only by living in accord with *ratio*. In *Satire* 5 true *libertas* (which can be identified and possessed only by a Stoic) versus false, or mere legal *libertas*, is a theme complementary to the proposal of *ratio*. Moderation (even of household resources) and freedom from avarice as rational qualities are among the first mentioned in P.5 as conducive to freedom and wisdom:

> es modicus voti, presso lare, dulcis amicis?
> iam nunc adstringas, iam nunc granaria laxes,
> inque luto fixum possis transcendere nummum
> nec gluttu sorbere salivam Mercurialem?
> "haec mea sunt, teneo" cum vere dixeris, esto
> liberque ac sapiens praetoribus ac Iove dextro. (5.109-14)

Legal liberty by no means ensures true liberty. Even freed, a slave, if not possessed of a rational mind, remains a slave. Note here again the concept of "internal masters," this time arising within a polluted ("sick") liver:

---

[12] Here again, "ear" is metaphorical *animus*, the receptacle of *ratio*.

> an dominum ignoras nisi quem vindicta relaxat?
> "i puer, et strigiles Crispini ad balnea defer."
> si increpuit, "cessas nugator?", servitium acre
> te nihil inpellit nec quicquam extrinsecus intrat
> quod nervos agitet; sed si intus et in iecore aegro
> nascuntur domini, quin tu impunitior exis
> atque hic quem ad strigiles scutica metus egit erilis? (5.125-31)

Carnal (sexual) slavery (cf. P.4.48, *si facis in penem quidquid tibi venit*) likewise precludes true *libertas*, as shown by the example of one who cannot cleanly extricate himself from a detrimental liaison:

> "quidnam igitur faciam? nec nunc, cum arcessat et ultro
> supplicet, accedam?" (5.172-73)

Wholeness and "integrity," qualities which accompany *ratio* and promote *libertas*, are stressed by P. in contrast again to mere social (legal) freedom:

> "si totus et integer illinc
> exieras, nec nunc." - hic, hic quod quaerimus, hic est,
> non in festuca, lictor quam iactat ineptus. (5.173-75)

A notable result of one's unwillingness to engage in introspection is a self-deception which manifests itself in assumed self-worth. Disillusionment about one's personal qualities in fact is a major theme in P.'s philosophical message. Note for example the voice of the Stoic censor at 3.27-29, a critical comment on the falsehood of illustrious ancestry:

> an deceat pulmonem rumpere ventis
> stemmata quod Tusco ramum millesime ducis
> censoremve tuum vel quod trabeate salutas?

Ancestral pretension as false basis for self-justification in fact contributes to the thematic foundation, as we have seen, of *Satire* 4, as does Alcibiades' superficial beauty. The Socratic/Stoic voice in *Satire 4* begins to illustrate Alcibiades' lack of actual philosophical understanding (as prerequisite to political leadership) almost immediately, sarcasm strengthening ironically the Alcibiadean paradox:

> scilicet ingenium et rerum prudentia velox
> ante pilos venit, dicenda tacendave calles. (4.4-5)

The point here (and throughout the mock-dialogue) is of course Alcibiades' total lack of philosophical competence. And again, P. allots the character of Alcibiades only the false defenses of surface beauty and illustrious ancestry:

> i nunc,
> "Dinomaches ego sum" suffla, "sum candidus." (4.19-20)

Yet P. also, as is seen by returning to *Satire* 3, posits a theory as to why the philosophically retarded tend to remain so: self-examination is to them terrifying. Virtue having been abandoned, it becomes painfully impossible to admit one's depravity:

> virtutem videant intabescantque relicta.
> anne magis Siculi gemuerunt aera iuvenci
> et magis auratis pendens laquearibus ensis
> purpureas subter cervices terruit, "imus,
> imus praecipites" quam si sibi dicat ... (3.38-42)

And, as concrete embodiment of philosophical retardation (and indeed illustrative of the kind of mis-guidance which even attacks philosophy), P. presents the centurion:

> dixeris haec inter varicosos centuriones,
> continuo crassum ridet Pulfenius ingens
> et centum Graecos curto centusse licetur. (5.189-91)

And:

> 'hic aliquis de gente hircosa centurionum
> dicat: 'quod sapio satis est mihi ...[13] (3.77-78)

And finally, to the centurion's anti-philosophical commentary, P. makes the "muscular youth" sympathize:

> his populus ridet, multumque torosa iuventus
> ingeminat tremulos naso crispante cachinnos. (3.86-87)

Key words of description in the above passage assist the characterization of the anti-intellectual(s). Centurions are "veiny" (*varicosos*, 5.189), implying also "strutting,

---

[13] Note that *sapio* here profits from *hircosa*; besides "know" or "understand," we can appreciate a pun with its meaning "taste." Thus the centurions are "goatish" too in that they, like goats, "know" little else but "what they eat."

swaggering" (cf. *varicare*).[14] Pulfenius is "massive" (*ingens*, 5.190), implying of course over-emphasis on the physical, atrophy of the mental. "Goatish" (*hircosa*, 3.77), applied to the entire "race" of centurions, suggests not only "smelly," but also all those other characteristics with which goats have always been associated: libidinousness, appetite, belligerence, etc. The young which sympathize with the centurion are likewise "bulging" (*torosa*, 3.86), again implying mental atrophy and animalistic brawn.[15] In sum, those represented by the centurions are contra-rational; their careless scorn is antithetical to the philosophical message presented in P.'s satires.

---

[14] As pointed out by Harvey (1981) 180, the adjective *varicosus* is satiric, occurring at Lucil. 801 (M); J. 6.397. It is indeed a term of abuse, not merely an explanation that varicosity "... was an occupational hazard of ancient soldiering ..." (Lee and Barr [1987] 156).

[15] *Torosus* is an adjective used more in association with animals than with humans. Cf. e.g., Col. 6.6.20: *tauris torosior cervix*.

1b. The Philosophical Message in Juvenal

In *Satire* 13, J. actually appears to make a personal statement about his philosophical tendencies. He is, in fact, an adherent to no single philosophical system, and even confounds the Stoics and Cynics; nor is his portrayal of Epicurus serious:

> Accipe quae contra valeat solacia ferre
> et qui nec Cynicos nec Stoica dogmata legit
> a Cynicis tunica distantia, non Epicurum
> suspicit exigui laetum plantaribus horti. (13.120-23)

J.'s point here is that formal philosophical doctrine is not the only provider of solace (*solacia*, 120). As we will see, J. even finds that philosophy (philosophers) has become subject, like other societal aspects, to corruption. In pointing out (or after merely hinting at) what he observes to be philosophical pretense, J. opens for himself a route to posit common sense, moderation, and life in accord with *Natura* as the most acceptable philosophical system.

As early as *Satire* 2, J. attacks false philosophers, in this case Stoics--Stoics in superficial form only, their philosophy a mask to cover their perverse nature:

> indocti primum, quamquam plena omnia gypso
> Chrysippi invenias; nam perfectissimus horum,
> si quis Aristotelen similem vel Pittacon emit
> et iubet archetypos pluteum servare Cleanthas.
> frontis nulla fides. (2.4-8)

And although J. will present Socrates as a model of moderation,[16] he points out the paradox which false philosophers embody by speaking of "Socratic *cinaedi*:"

> castigas turpia, cum sis
> inter Socraticos notissima fossa cinaedos? (2.9-10)

And again, although J. will uphold and promote the (Stoic) concept of *Virtus*,[17] he mentions it along with the (homosexual) "ass-shaking" of the false Stoics (*Stoicidae*)[18] to underline their hypocrisy:

---

[16] At 14.319-21.
[17] E.g., at 8.19-20.
[18] J.'s false philosophers become *trepidi* ... *Stoicidae* at 2.64-5 following Laronia's exposure of their perverse hypocrisy. Another notable denunciation of a Stoic is delivered by Umbricius (3.114-18).

> ... de virtute locuti
> clunem agitant. (2.20-21)

As close as J. ever comes to approving of actual adherents to Stoicism is his citation of Zeno as anti-cannibalistic. But this case of course serves primarily to offer to the Cantabrians a mock-excuse[19] for their cannibalism, since no Stoic was to be found there:

> melius nos
> Zenonis praecepta monent, nec enim omnia, quaedam
> pro vita facienda putant; sed Cantaber unde
> Stoicus, antiqui praesertim aetate Metelli? (15.106-09)

Yet despite J.'s citation of (pseudo-)Stoics as corrupt or inconsequential, J. repeatedly calls for *ratio* and *virtus*, or at least stresses in many cases the tendency to ignore them. Two examples from *Satire* 10 will suffice to illustrate this. Here J. implies that both human fears and desires are irrational:

> quid enim ratione timemus
> aut cupimus? (10.4-5)

And here, in connection with a discourse on prayer (i.e. what one should, should not wish for), J. presents *virtus* as the "only sure path to a tranquil life," and at once stresses that it is strictly an inner quality:

> monstro quod ipse tibi possis dare; semita certe
> tranquillae per virtutem patet unica vitae. (10.363-64)

In J.'s view, however, *virtus* has been overshadowed by materialism or the desire for fame. "Virtue" itself is, in J.'s presentation of society, pursued only as a means to immediate rewards:

> tanto maior famae sitis est quam
> virtutis. quis enim virtutem amplectitur ipsam,
> praemia si tollas? (10.140-42)

Although in reference to historical persons/events (see e.g., Ferguson [1979] 144), Umbricius' attack is part of an overall denunciation of Greeks in general.

[19] That J. is sarcastic here is indicated too by his apparent factual inaccuracy. In citing evidence that Stoic doctrine did not strictly forbid cannibalism, Ferguson (1979) 319 states that "J obviously did not know this."

Virtus is also a key concept in J.'s distinction between true and feigned *nobilitas* in *Satire* 8. *Stemmata* ("pedigrees," 1) *per se* lend nothing to the acquisition of *nobilitas*, asserts J. in his opening address to a certain Ponticus. At 8.19-20 J. contrasts "old waxen (images)" as display of *nobilitas* with *virtus*, without which all is empty pretense:[20]

> tota licet veteres exornent undique cerae
> atria, nobilitas sola est atque unica virtus.

No one, in J.'s eyes, is worthy of acknowledgement as leader unless "good (qualities) of the soul" lead him to proper speech and deed. J.'s philosophic message therefore (like that of P.) includes the distinction between actual and assumed self-worth:

> prima mihi debes animi bona, sanctus haberi
> iustitiaeque tenax factis dictisque mereris?
> agnosco procerem. (8.24-6)

As example of false self-assertion of nobility J. introduces ostensibly one Rubellius Blandus, whose response to the satirist's criticism recalls that of P.'s Alcibiades:

> "vos humiles," inquis, "volgi pars ultima nostri,
> quorum nemo queat patriam monstrare parentis;
> ast ego Cecropides." (8.44-6)

Yet J. turns the "Cecropid's" boast against him. He is, in fact, merely a living "image"-- an image distinct from a truncated herm only in that his head is of flesh, not stone:

>   at tu
> nil nisi Cecropides, truncoque simillimus Hermae:
> nullo quippe alio vincis discrimine quam quod
> illi marmoreum caput est, tua vivit imago. (8.52-5)

J. continues in *Satire* 8, by illustration of historical exempla, to strengthen the dichotomy of real versus assumed nobility. Nobles in name who actually proved disgraceful in deed are presented first. Nero paraded as a cithara-player (*res haut mira tamen citharoedo principe mimus/nobilis*, 198-99). Gracchus posed as a gladiator (*movet ecce tridentem*, 203). The civil traitors Catiline and Cethegus were of noble parentage

---

[20] Just as in P., *ambitio* is mentioned by J. as anti-virtuous:
    quod si praecipitem rapit ambitio atque libido. (8.135)

(*quid, Catilina, tuis natalibus atque Cethegi/inveniet quisquam sublimius?*, 231-32). In contrast to these exempla are then listed "base-born" who proved noble in deed. Cicero was not originally a noble Roman, having been born at Arpinum (*hic novus Arpinas, ignobilis et modo Romae/municipalis eques*, 237-38). Gaius Marius worked the farm of another (... *in monte solebat/poscere mercedes alieno lassus aratro*, 245-46). The Decii were plebeian in origin (*plebeiae Deciorum animae, plebeia fuerunt/nomina*, 254-55). Rome's "last of the good kings," Servius Tullius, was no more than a handmaid's son (*ancilla natus trabeam et diadema Quirini/et fascis meruit, regum ultimus ille bonorum*, 259-60).

Among other philosophical themes which P. and J. share is that of trade as symptomatic of the corruption of the soul by avarice. J.14.256-302 is a summary of the practice of trade and the perils involved therein. The trader's craft is pointless, asserts J., because the perils of sea-travel greatly outweigh the value of the trade-goods. Thus the trader himself is "lost and base," his merchandise "smelly:"

> perditus ac vilis sacci mercator olentis,
> qui gaudes pingue antiquae de litore Cretae
> passum et municipes Iovis advexisse lagonas? (14.269-71)

Greed causes the trader to deny reality (risking death), and the money he seeks is described in immaterial terms:

> "nil color hic caeli, nil fascia nigra minantur."

And:

> concisum argentum in titulos faciesque minutas. (14.291)

And finally J. describes the end which will eventually meet the avaricious; ironically, he will end up with nothing, a beggar:

> sed cuius votis modo non suffecerat aurum
> quod Tagus et rutila volvit Pactolus harena,
> frigida sufficient velantes inguina panni
> exiguusque cibus, mersa rate naufragus assem
> dum rogat et picta se tempestate tuetur. (14.298-302)

The philosophy which J. presents in *Satire* 14 (by which excessive greed can be avoided) interestingly involves amalgamation of the convictions of the Cynics (Diogenes), Epicurus, and Socrates. In contrast to the "lofty villas" of a Cretonius (... *alta parabat/culmina villarum*, 88-9) J. praises the absolute practicality of the Cynic's jar:

>   dolia nudi
> non ardent Cynici; si fregeris, altera fiet
> cras domus, atque eadem plumbo commissa manebit. (14.308-10)

Epicurus, Socrates, *natura* and *sapientia* all dictate rational moderation:

> quantum, Epicure, tibi parvis suffecit in hortis,
> quantum Socratici ceperunt ante penates;
> numquam aliud natura, aliud sapientia dicit. (14.319-21)

Contrast the philosophical models of Epicurus and Socrates with J.'s modern victim of avarice:

> longa tibi posthac fato meliore dabuntur,
> si tantum culti solus possederis agri
> quantum sub Tatio populus Romanus arabat. (14.158-60)

What sufficed for the entire Roman population in early history is now sought after by a single immoderate, indicating the dichotomy between early history and the present (and suggesting the difference in the philosophical outlooks of past and present Romans).

Also presented by J. are symbols of contrasting philosophies. Although J. asserts that in Democritus of Abdera's time society was less absurd than that of the present, he commends his ridicule. The description of Democritus even reminds us of J.'s own satiric program, since the philosopher, like J., found absurdity in virtually every human activity; cares, joys, even tears provided material for laughter:

> tunc quoque materiam risus invenit ad omnis
> occursus hominum. (10.47-8)

And:

> ridebat curas nec non et gaudia vulgi,
> interdum et lacrimas. (10.51-2)

Heraclitus of Ephesus (the *contrarius auctor* of 10.30) is not the satirist's philosopher, since he greets human folly not with laughter, but with tears:

> sed facilis cuivis rigidi censura cachinni:
> mirandum est unde ille oculis suffecerit umor. (10.31-2)

J. cites throughout his satires a complex amalgam of philosophical doctrines and maxims,[21] although, as we have seen, he professes to be an adherent to no specific system. Anger and ignorance are qualities displayed by those with no philosophical conscience; *sapientia* (13.189), however, "teaches right," whether it be that of the Stoics, the ancient Thales, or Socrates:

> Chrysippus non dicet idem nec mite Thaletis
> ingenium dulcique senex vicinus Hymetto,
> qui partem acceptae saeva inter vincla cicutae
> accusatori nollet dare. plurima felix
> paulatim vitia atque errores exuit, omnes
> prima docens rectum, sapientia.[22] (13.184-89)

Perhaps the key to J.'s overall philosophical message can be found at 13.19-22, ostensibly part of a consolation to Corvinus for having been defrauded:

> magna quidem, sacris quae dat praecepta libellis,
> victrix fortunae sapientia, ducimus autem
> hos quoque felices, qui ferre incommoda vitae
> nec iactare iugum vita didicere magistra.

J. admits the didactic value of philosophy (*sapientia*), especially its ability to "conquer fortune." But philosophy resides primarily in books (*libellis*) in the form of mere precepts (*praecepta*). Yet it is "life's instructor" (*vita ... magistra*) which is set along side *sapientia* as able to guide one along a tranquil existence (*nec iactare iugum*). Thus J. sees the extremity of strict philosophical doctrine, just as he observes the extremity of the behavior of those who lack rationality altogether.

---

[21] To mention only three minor examples: the Delphic γνῶθι σεαυτόν (11.27); the Epicurean *voluptates commendat rarior usus* (11.208; cf. Epictetus, *Flor.* 6.59); Pythagorean vegetarianism: *Pythagoras, cunctis animalibus abstinuit qui* (15.173).

[22] Presumably perplexed to encounter such a general philosophical statement in J., at least one ed. deletes 13.187-89; cf. Clausen's apparatus: "plurima - sapientia *del. Guyet.*" However, 13.19-22 (which Clausen does not bracket) argue against deletion of 13.187-89.

2. Society, Politics, Religion in Persius

We have seen that Rome, indeed virtually everyone at Rome, is presented by P. as "disordered" (*turbida*, 1.5); Rome itself is likewise "reprobate" (*improbum*, 1.6). In such a society, one's only salvation is to be self-reliant, to become as it were an island (*... nec te quaesiveris extra*, 1.7). This assessment, while ostensibly in reference specifically to the literary sphere, complements P.'s view of the (larger) sphere of society and politics. Corruption of the legal system is a facet of the socio-political disease introduced as early as *Satire* 1:

> "fur es" ait Pedio. Pedius quid? crimina rasis
> librat in antithetis, doctas posuisse figuras
> laudatur: "bellum hoc." hoc bellum? an, Romule, ceves? (1.85-87)

The reality of crime is meaningless; style and presentation obscure even a simple and straight-forward accusation ("*fur es*,'"85). By his use of Romulus as metonymy for Rome, P. highlights the depth of Roman corruption--a corruption which extends down to the city's very foundation. Socio-political integrity has become perverted; the nerveless legal system's only response to crime is to "shake its ass (pathically)" (*ceves*, 87), inviting judicial buggery.

Political pretense is emphasized also by P. in *Satire* 1. Again here reality of importance versus mere appearance (style) is implied:

> sese aliquem credens Italo quod honore supinus
> fregerit heminas Arreti aedilis iniquas. (1.129-30)

P.'s aedile is "bent backwards" (*supinus*, 129),[23] perhaps, in P.'s perverse world, even pathically. "Italian office" (*Italo ... honore*, 129) indicates that corruption extends beyond the city of Rome, even in the most trivial of circumstances.

---

[23] *Supinus* of course suggests "proud" or "arrogant" in this context, but its other implications will not escape the attentive reader, especially given the homosexual imagery already presented. Cf. e.g., the image of the aedile "on his back," prostituting himself to gain political office.

P.'s "nobles" likewise embody pretense, a pretense which naturally requires hypocrisy. In contrast to P.'s Macrinus, "a good portion of the nobles" (*bona pars procerum*, 2.5) are hypocritical, pretending modest nobility, yet victims of greed:

> "mens bona, fama, fides", haec clara et ut audiat hospes;
> illa sibi introrsum et sub lingua murmurat: "o si
> sub rastro crepet argenti mihi seria dextro
> Hercule! pupillumve utinam, quem proximus heres
> inpello, expugnam; nam et est scabiosus et acri
> bile tumet. Nerio iam tertia conditur uxor." (2.8-14)

The above passage illustrates well P.'s recurrent theme of appearance versus reality; what is presented (e.g., by the noble[s]) to society openly masks a cryptic wish for material gain. Gain, in P.'s picture of Roman society, is in fact all important. Indeed, as we have seen, greed has prevented individual members of society in general from knowing even their "station in life" (... *humana qua parte locatus es in re*, 3.67).

Partially of course as an aid to his philosophical message concerning true freedom, yet in part also to point out the artificial arbitrariness of societal structure, P. comments on the process of citizenship. A Roman citizen is created merely by the cap of Quirinus:

> at illum
> hesterni capite induto subiere Quirites. (3.105-06)

Citizenship is awarded not out of merit, but arbitrarily, and P. implies that it is only natural therefore that the Roman citizenry are 'civil' only nominally. Even a known liar (*mendax*, 5.77) gains (false) credit by the ritual of citizenship:

> heu steriles veri, quibus una Quiritem
> vertigo facit! hic Dama est non tresis agaso,
> vappa lippus et in tenui farragine mendax.
> verterit hunc dominus, momento turbinis[24] exit
> Marcus Dama. (5.75-79)

Crucial to P.'s socio-political message is the idea that the public and the politician live on a basis of perverse symbiosis. The politician is blatantly mercenary, yet the public

---

[24] *Turbinis* here reminds us of P.'s disparaging term for the Roman citizenry at large: *turbida Roma*.

encourages this quality with flattery.[25] Again, this is made explicit by the example of the politician extraordinaire, Alcibiades:

> quin tu igitur summa nequiquam pelle decorus
> ante diem blando caudam iactare popello
> desinis, Anticyras melior sorbere meracas? (4.14-16)

And the politician's mercenary nature is equal to that of an herb-seller:

> "'Dinomaches ego sum' suffla, 'sum candidus.' esto,
> dum ne deterius sapiat pannucia Baucis,
> cum bene discincto cantaverit ocima vernae." (4.20-22)

In short, P.'s politician is he who can, by material indulgence, win the favor and memory of the mob:

> "vigila et cicer ingere large
> rixanti populo, nostra ut floralia possint
> aprici meminisse senes." (5.177-79)

And, for the indiscriminate rapacity of the populace, 6.50-51:

> oleum artocreasque popello
> largior.

Thus we are presented with a Persian portrait of a Rome the socio-political status of which is determined by reciprocal rapacity. Honor is bestowed on political hopefuls by a society whose only concern lies in material gain. P.'s common citizen is possessed of an incurable illness: limitless avarice, such as that described at 6.78-80:

> rem duplica. "feci; iam triplex, iam mihi quarto,
> iam decies redit in rugam. depunge ubi sistam,
> inventus, Chrysippe, tui finitor acervi."

---

[25] The social intermediate between the populace and politician (the centurion-class) is, as we have seen, likewise depicted by P. as animalistically mindless (cf. 3.77-87; 5.189-91).

2b. Society, Politics, Religion in Juvenal

Just as P.'s societal greed manifests itself in a perverse and corrupt political system, so too does greed prevail in J.'s initial portrait of Roman society. "Nobility," chewed away (*nobilitate comesa*, 1.34), "infamy" and greed prevail (*quid enim salvis infamia nummis?*, 1.48). Political and social mobility are gained at the expense of honesty (*probitas laudatur et alget*, 1.74). It is through crime therefore that society prospers:

> criminibus debent hortos praetoria mensas,
> argentum vetus et stantem extra pocula caprum. (1.75-76)

Indeed the very name of political office has become perverse; those high on the *cursus honorum* even grovel for the *sportula* along with the common *plebs*:

> iubet a praecone vocari
> ipsos Troiugenas, nam vexant et limen et ipsi
> nobiscum. "da praetori, da deinde tribuno." (1.99-101)

In sum, J.'s society displays an almost inverted order wherein social status is determined not by legitimate honor or nobility, but rather by wealth alone. Money is all-important and lends authoritative audacity even to (foreign) freedmen:

> sed libertinus prior est. "prior" inquit "ego adsum.
> cur timeam dubitemve locum defendere, quamvis
> natus ad Euphraten, molles quod in aure fenestrae
> arguerint, licet ipse negem? sed quinque tabernae
> quadraginta parant." (1.102-06)

Wealth is no less than an agent of societal paradox. He who came to Rome as a slave (*pedibus ... albis*, 1.111) supercedes one holding "sacred office" (*sacro ... honori*, 1.110), this purely by the power of riches (*divitiae*, 1.109):

> expectent ergo tribuni,
> vincant divitiae, sacro ne cedat honori
> nuper in hanc urbem pedibus qui venerat albis. (1,109-111)

And for the corruption perceived by J. in Roman society there is no hope of improvement. Although "every vice is at its zenith," the future promises nothing different. J. offers to society a dim prognosis:

> Nil erit ulterius quod nostris moribus addat

> posteritas, eadem facient cupientque minores,
> omne in praecipiti vitium stetit. (1.147-49)

Unlike P., whose (programmatic) outline of societal ills stresses first the faults of the literary sphere, J. (even in his program) presents Roman society as a virtual nest of of diverse ills. As we have observed, J.'s Rome too is generally imbalanced (*nam quis iniquae/tam patiens urbis* ..., 1.30-31). Likewise, again in J.'s program, lack of complete freedom of expression in Rome is insinuated. J.'s reference to Tigellinus recalls Neronian society; the implicit suggestion is that post-Neronian Rome is no more free (safe) for the outspoken:

> pone Tigellinum: taeda lucebis in illa
> qua stantes ardent qui fixo gutture fumant,
> et latum media sulcum deducis harena. (1.155-57)

In connection with this (as we have observed), J. then presents an overt statement that he will attack only the dead (implied, however, is an attack on the living--the dead are emblematic):

> experiar quid concedatur in illos
> quorum Flaminia tegitur cinis atque Latina. (1.170-71)

Legality and politics likewise are for J.'s Rome (just as for P.'s) perverse. P.'s law-court reveals its femininity and lack of vigor through its obsequiousness (to one who delivers a poetic defense). J.'s court-officials are themselves clearly effeminate. Note here the paradox stressed by "harsh and unyielding" (*acer et indomitus*, 2.77) in combination with "(transparent) gauze" (*multicia*, 2.76):

> quid non proclames, in corpore iudicis ista
> si videas? quaero an deceant multicia testem.[26]
> acer et indomitus libertatisque magister,
> Cretice, perluces. (2.75-78)

Further, J. implies an historical evolution of Roman perversity. His example of Gracchus serves to illustrate a gradual political decline:

---

[26] The pun on *testem* has been noted. Ferguson (1979) 130: "... a formal witness and the male sex-organ."

> Quadraginta dedit Gracchus sestertia dotem
> cornicini, sive hic recto cantaverit aere. (2.116-17)

And:

> Vicit et hoc monstrum tunicati fuscina Gracchi,
> lustravitque fuga mediam gladiator harenam
> et Capitolinis generosior et Marcellis
> et Catuli Pauliique minoribus et Fabiis et
> omnibus ad podium spectantibus, his licet ipsum
> admoveas cuius tunc munere retia misit. (2.143-48)

And J. concludes his socio-political message in *Satire* 2 with the ironic comment that even conquered Armenians are made corrupt (perverse) by victorious Rome:

> aspice quid faciant commercia: venerat obses,
> hic fiunt homines. nam si mora longior urbem
> indulsit pueris, non umquam derit amator.
> mittentur bracae, cultelli, frena, flagellum:
> sic praetextatos referunt Artaxata mores. (2.166-70)

Although the words of Umbricius display indignant exaggeration (making him slightly self-defacing), they convey no less than a universal indictment of the urban condition. In a summary statement on Rome (3.21-25), stressed are dishonesty, the futility of (honest) work, and poverty:

> Hic tunc Umbricius "quando artibus," inquit, "honestis
> nullus in urbe locus, nulla emolumenta laborum,
> res hodie minor est here quam fuit atque eadem cras
> deteret exiguis aliquid, proponimus illuc
> ire, fatigatas ubi Daedalus exuit alas.

Umbricius' socio-political critique of Rome depends on a rather categorical scheme, wherein at least nine distinct aspects can be identified:

1. Fortune's favor raises societal dregs, and this leads to a perverse abuse of wealth:

> quondam hi cornicines et municipalis harenae
> perpetui comites notaeque per oppida buccae
> munera nunc edunt et, verso pollice vulgus
> cum iubet, occidunt populariter; inde reversi
> conducunt foricas, et cur non omnia? cum sint
> quales ex humili magna ad fastigia rerum
> extollit quotiens voluit Fortuna iocari. (3.34-40)

Wealth gained by these "horn-blowers" is perversely employed in death for public amusement and sewer-work. The "son of free-born parents" must give way to a "rich man's slave," the kind who will not hesitate to dispense a legion's wage for a brief encounter with a whore (although Umbricius implies that he would do likewise if able):[27]

>   divitis hic servo cludit latus ingenuorum
>   filius; alter enim quantum in legione tribuni
>   accipiunt donat Calvinae vel Catienae,
>   ut semel aut iterum super illam palpitet; at tu,
>   cum tibi vestiti facies scorti placet, haeres
>   et dubitas alta Chionen deducere sella. (3.131-36)

2. Political corruption prevails, bringing with it hypocrisy:

>   me nemo ministro
>   fur erit, atque ideo nulli comes exeo tamquam
>   mancus et extinctae corpus non utile dextrae.
>   quis nunc diligitur nisi conscius et cui fervens
>   aestuat occultis animus semperque tacendis? (3.46-50)

And only wealth lends credibility:[28]

>   da testem Romae tam sanctum quam fuit hospes
>   numinis Idaei, procedat vel Numa vel qui
>   servavit trepidam flagranti ex aede Minervam:
>   protinus ad censum, de moribus ultima fiet
>   quaestio. "quot pascit servos? quot possidet agri
>   iugera? quam multa magnaque paropside cenat?"
>   quantum quisque sua nummorum servat in arca,
>   tantum habet et fidei. iures licet et Samothracum
>   et nostrorum aras, contemnere fulmina pauper
>   creditur atque deos dis ignoscentibus ipsis. (3.137-46)

3. Symptomatic of societal corruption and greed also stands blackmail:

---

[27] Abuse of wealth by the 'sub-plebeian' who have become wealthy is a recurrent theme in J. Cf. e.g., 4.23-5; 31-3:

>   hoc tu
>   succinctus patria quondam, Crispine, papyro?
>   hoc pretio squamae?
>
>   purpureus magni ructarit scurra Palati,
>   iam princeps equitum, magna qui voce solebat
>   vendere municipes fracta de merce siluros?

[28] The motif of (ex)slaves as bearers of false witness occurs similarly at 7.13-16:

>   hoc satius quam si dicas sub iudice "vidi"
>   quod non vidisti; faciant equites Asiani,
>   [quamquam et Cappadoces faciant equitesque Bithyni]
>   altera quos nudo traducit gallica talo.

> nil tibi se debere putat, nil conferet umquam,
> participem qui te secreti fecit honesti. (3.49-52)

4. Exemplifying items 1, 2 and 3 above are invasive Greeks. Verses 3.58-125 place at least some of the blame for Rome's societal decline upon them specifically, and their influence is described as "poison" able to cause the (honest) Roman to be displaced:

> nam cum facilem stillavit in aurem
> exiguum de naturae patriaeque veneno,
> limine summoveor. (3.122-24)

5. And, although (again) Umbricius seems to suggest that he too would engage in legacy-hunting were it not for overly-intense competition, this practice too is naturally symptomatic of corruption and greed:

> quod porro officium, ne nobis blandiar, aut quod
> pauperis hic meritum, si curet nocte togatus
> currere, cum praetor lictorem inpellat et ire
> praecipitem iubeat dudum vigilantibus orbis,
> ne prior Albinam et Modiam collega salutet? (3.126-30)

6. The massive rift between rich and poor is described by Umbricius at 3.147-89. This is summed up at 3.183-4: *omnia Romae/cum pretio*. This financial rift is then illustrated by example at 3.203-22, where Cordus [owner of "nothing" (*nihil*, 209)] is contrasted with Asturicus and Persicus ["duly suspected of arson" (*... et merito iam/suspectus tamquam ipse suas incenderit aedes*, 221-2)].

7. Umbricius' eulogy of rusticity is preceded by a vivid exposé of ruin, fire, and exorbitant rents (this at 3.190-202).[29] Rome is in fact on the verge of collapse, yet this fact is disguised [certainly Umbricius' description of the "masking of gaping cracks" (*veteris rimae cum texit hiatum,/securos pendente iubet dormire ruina*, 195-6) applies not

---

[29] Note on 3.198-9 (J.'s reference to Ucagleon) echoes of Vergil. Comm. have noted this allusion to the Vergilian character (e.g., Ferguson [1979] 149, who interprets it thus: "You - the ordinary Roman - are the modern Aeneas, descendant of the founder - only *you* won't be able to escape."). The Ucagleon-allusion also recalls, however, Umbricius' massive anti-Greek diatribe, since Vergil's passage (incl. A. 2.311) is actually Aeneas' account of the invasion of Troy by the Greeks, who had just deceived the Trojans with the wooden horse. In fact, Aeneas' whole speech in Book 2 is about the destruction of a city by invading Greeks; so too is much of Umbricius'.

only to single buildings, but metaphorically to the entire city in all its aspects]. One must essentially quit Rome, escaping the (antithetical) hazards of fire and darkness:

> vivendum est illic, ubi nulla incendia, nulli
> nocte metus. (3.197-8)

Umbricius finally opts for the rustic existence; for the rent of "shadows" one might purchase a country villa. The call is to agriculture; "loving the spade," one may find consolation in a small, cultivated garden:

> si potes avelli circensibus, optima Sorae
> aut Fabrateriae domus aut Frusinone paratur
> quanti nunc tenebras unum conducis in annum.
> hortulus hic puteusque brevis nec reste movendus
> in tenuis plantas facili diffunditur haustu.
> vive bidentis amans et culti vilicus horti
> unde epulum possis centum dare Pythagoreis. (3.223-29)

8. Overcrowding brings concomitant noise-pollution. The (exaggerated) picture presented is that people even die from lack of sleep (*plurimus hic aeger moritur vigilando*, 232); again, only the wealthy are at ease in Rome (*magnis opibus dormitur in urbe*, 235). In the overcrowded streets, Umbricius is literally "battered" (*ferit hic cubito, ferit assere duro/alter, at hic tignum capiti incutit, ille meretram*, 245-6).

9. Finally are nominated the various "*pericula noctis*" (268). These include specifically litter falling from high windows (*quod spatium tectis sublimibus unde cerebrum testa ferit; rimosa et curta fenestris/vasa cadant*, 269-71); belligerent muggers (*ebrius ac petulans, qui nullum forte cecidit,/dat poenas*, 278-9); burglery and personal crime generally abound (*grassator agit rem*, 305).

The speech of Umbricius aside, we will see, in the discussion of J.'s religious message (esp. re. *Sat.* 10), that wealth (or rather the quest therefor) has supplanted traditional (religious) values. Wealth (*Fortuna*) has, in J.'s commentary, in fact become Rome's governing divinity.

Like P., J. sees political status as subject to the will of a fickle public. Sejanus' political fate is described by J. as an example:

> iam strident ignes, iam follibus atque caminis
> ardet adoratum populo caput et crepat ingens
> Seianus, deinde ex facie toto orbe secunda
> fiunt urceoli, pelves, sartago, matellae. (10.61-4)

Similarly, J.'s Roman public is a fickle and uncritical "mob," knowing only the impetus of wealth:

> sed quid
> turba Remi? sequitur fortunam, ut semper, et odit
> damnatos. idem populus, si Nortia Tusco
> favisset, si oppressa foret secura senectus
> principis, hac ipsa Seianum diceret hora
> Augustum. (10.72-7)

Further, (political) glory after death is mere illusion:[30]

> patriam tamen obruit olim
> gloria paucorum et laudis titulique cupido
> haesuri saxis cinerum custodibus, ad quae
> discutienda valent sterilis mala robora fici,
> quandoquidem data sunt ipsis quoque fata sepulcris. (10.142-46)

Also on the topic of politicians, J. describes a decline in quality from past to present. Social leaders of old were more honest and noble than their modern counterparts. Even the Roman Senate of old, in its most luxurious indulgence, was simple, dining on common farm-fare: *haedulus* (11.66), *montani/asparagi* (68-9), *ova ... cum matribus* (71), *uvae* (72), *pirum* (73), *mala* (74); *Haec olim nostri iam luxuriosa senatus/cena fuit* (77-8). One serving as consul and dictator was modest, even not above tilling the soil (*erectum domito referens a monte ligonem*, 11.89).

Conversely, J.'s modern political leaders are no better than the mob they govern; all are concerned only with public games (*totam hodie Romam circus capit*, 11.197).

---

[30] Even the military and political accomplishments of Hannibal and Alexander the Great amount to nothing in the end in J.'s presentation. Hannibal is *demens*, 10.166; Alexander is *infelix*, 10.169, and will be forced to settle with the space of a tomb in lieu of world conquest (*sarcophago contentus erit*, 10.172).

Even the praetor is "booty of nags," although in triumphal honor (*similisque triumpho/praeda caballorum praetor sedet*, 194-5).[31]

In connection with the socio-political messages of P. and J., it is necessary to address the topic of religiosity. P.'s first critique of (false) religious practice appears in *Satire* 2, wherein "a good part of the leaders of society" (*bona pars procerum*, 5) are exposed as (religiously) hypocritical. Indeed, hardly anyone at Rome (*haut cuivis*, 6) is willing "to live with open prayer" (*aperto vivere voto*, 7). With "silent incense" (*tacita ... acerra*, 5) do the *proceres* pray for wealth; openly the wish is for good faith, reputation and mind:

> "mens bona, fama, fides" haec clara et ut audiat hospes;
> illa sibi introsum et sub lingua murmurat: "o si
> ebulliat patruus, praeclarum funus!" (2.8-10)

And even if one should wish only for health in old age (instead of ill-gained wealth), excess and self-indulgence preclude even Jove:

> Poscis opem nervis corpusque fidele senectae.
> esto, age; sed grandes patinae tuccetaque crassa
> adnuere his superos vetuere Iovemque morantur. (2.41-3)

Personal greed yields a perverse impression of the gods. Since, asserts P., all are motivated by bribery and avarice, so too do they attribute these characteristics even to deities.[32] Thus religion has become a perversion wherein the benificence of the gods is expected in return only for riches:

> hinc illud subiit, auro sacras quod ovato
> perducis facies. "nam fratres inter aevos,
> somnia pituita qui purgatissima mittunt,
> praecipui sunto sitque illis aurea barba."
> aurum vasa Numae Saturniaque inpulit aera

---

[31] In *Sat. 6* J. presents a similar dichotomy between pre-historic and modern womankind. In the contemporary society of J., adultery is rampant (6.76-7; 80-1). Promiscuity leads to abortion (6.595-7). Again, the advent of *luxuria* is responsible for the corruption of women (6.293).

[32] Indeed in *Sat.* 6 the joke is made that to one hoping for money, even a potential benefactor becomes a god:
> sum tibi Mercurius; venio deus huc ego ut ille
> pingitur. (6.62-3)

> Vestalisque urnas et Tuscum fictile mutat. (2.55-60)

In contrast, honest and modest prayer can be realized for the price of "grits:"

> haec cedo ut admoveam templis, et farre litabo. (2.75)

J.'s picture of religion at Rome is likewise perverse. Specifically, the ceremony of the *Bona Dea* is inverted by "reversed custom" (*more sinistro*, 2.87). In this case a religious rite is taken advantage of by men who would be women, the exclusivity of the *Bona Dea* worship only affording further opportunity for imagined feminism:[33]

> atque bonam tenerae placant abdomine porcae
> et magno cratere deam. sed more sinistro
> exagitata procul non intrat femina limen:
> solis ara deae maribus patet. "ite, profanae,"
> clamatur, "nullo gemit hic tibicina cornu." (2.86-90)

Even J.'s religious guardians (representatives) are corrupt. A vestal virgin allows herself lovers:

> incestus, cum quo nuper vittata iacebat
> sanguine adhuc vivo terram subitura sacerdos?[34] (4.9-10)

Irreverent behavior is in fact promoted by foreign religiosity, and this is therefore pursued by the licentious. Note for example 6.535-8:

> ille petit veniam, quotiens non abstinet uxor
> concubitu sacris observandisque diebus
> magnaque debetur violato poena cadurco
> et movisse caput visa est argentea serpens.

Traditional religion has in fact been supplanted by superstition, the instigators of which are of course (mercenary) foreigners.[35] Yet the mercenary nature of Roman religion itself is made explicit by J. The "primary and most well-known prayer" is for wealth:

---

[33] Cf. for the decline of traditional religiosity and the violation of the rites of the *Bona Dea* 6.342-5:
> et quis tunc hominum contemptor numinis, aut quis
> simpuvium ridere Numae nigrumque catinum
> et Vaticano fragiles de monte patellas
> ausus erat? sed nunc ad quas non Clodius aras?

[34] Ferguson (1979) 160 traces J.'s reference to "the notorious case of Cornelia, the senior Vestal Virgin ... who was convicted in AD 91 of breaking her vows of chastity."

[35] Note the stress on religious (superstitious) exoticism imparted by e.g., 6.540-55: *Osiris* (541), *Iudaea* (543), *Solymarum* (544), *Iudaei* (547), *Armenius*, *Commagenus* (550), *Chaldaeis* (553), *Hammonis*, *Delphis* (555).

> prima fere vota et cunctis notissima templis
> divitiae, crescant ut opes, ut maxima toto
> nostra sit arca foro. (10.23-5)

Satire 10 is naturally J.'s most religion-oriented--no less than an exposition on what should and should not be prayed for. Before J. posits an opinion as to what one should request from the gods, he outlines what are more or less standard prayers and then illustrates their futility. Eloquence and fame (*eloquium ac famam*, 114), such as that of a Demosthenes or a Cicero, are perils to the possessor (*eloquio sed uterque perit orator*, 118). Old age realized is a curse (*sed quam continuis et quantis longa senectus/plena malis!*, 190-1). Beauty for one's children is likewise pernicious (*formam optat modico pueris, maiore puellis/murmure*, 289-90), since it will only ensure their corruption (*rara est adeo concordia formae/atque pudicitiae*, 297-8). J.'s (pessimistic) religious conclusion is that man, by his mis-guided prayers, works his own destruction--the gods in fact display more concern for mankind than he does himself (*carior est illis homo quam sibi*, 350). J. recommends therefore only a modest prayer: *orandum est ut sit mens sana in corpore sano* (356).

Yet the common tendency for excessive prayer (in contrast to J.'s votive modesty) is complemented in *Satire* 13 by a depiction of the modern pantheon as itself excessive. The Roman world's theocracy has deteriorated from the time when Saturn reigned:

> nulla super nubes convivia caelicolarum
> nec puer Iliacus formonsa nec Herculis uxor
> ad cyathos et iam siccato nectare tergens
> bracchia Volcanus Liparaea nigra taberna;
> prandebat sibi quisque deus nec turba deorum
> talis ut est hodie, contentaque sidera paucis
> numinibus miserum urguebant Atlanta minori
> pondere; nondum imi sortitus triste profundi
> imperium Sicula torvos cum coniuge Pluton,
> nec rota nec Furiae nec saxum aut volturis atri
> poena, sed infernis hilares sine regibus umbrae. (13.42-52)

Even those who believe in the gods avoid divine law, asserts J. Criminality as means to (financial) prosperity is for them too attractive; divine retribution seems slow and inconsistent:

> "ut sit magna, tamen certe lenta ira deorum est;
> si curant igitur cunctos punire nocentes,
> quando ad me venient? sed et exorabile numen
> fortasse experiar; solet his ignoscere. multi
> committunt eadem diverso crimina fato:
> ille crucem sceleris pretium tulit, hic diadema." (13.100-05)

Greed has so greatly overshadowed reverence in Rome that for wealth the avaricious will literally turn the gods into gain:

> haec ibi si non sunt, minor extat sacrilegus qui
> radat inaurati femur Herculis et faciem ipsam
> Neptuni, qui brattoleam de Castore ducat;
> an dubitet solitus totum conflare Tonantem?[36] (13.150-53)

---

[36] V. 153, bracketed in Clausen's text, has been suspected of being either corrupt or an interpolation, since it appears a contradiction that a "petty irreverent" (*minor sacrilegus*) could be "accustomed" (*solitus*) to commit the major sacriligious crime of demolishing a statue of Jove. Yet this may be (typical) Juvenalian ironic exaggeration, and the suggested emendation of *solitus* to *solitumst*, while attractive (see e.g. Courtney [1980] 553), seems unnecessary.

3. Interrelationships of Form, Style and Meaning in Persius

In the previous chapters (and here too so far) I have constructed and suggested the (meaningful) intentions of P. and J.--intentions in program, voice (persona), and language. Yet semantic aspects of these intentions are of course interdependent. Form (more so compositional style) is a conscious construct. Form too assists meaning; meaning in turn, while derivative of form, is its directive. The question which then poses itself, and which must be confronted, is this: Is P. or J. concerned more with (poetic) aesthetics or with (socio-philosophical) ethics?[37] Or, to rephrase this question, how does form relate to meaning? Consider P. first.

The question of P.'s aestheticism is complicated by the fact that much of P.'s satiric message is directed precisely at contemporary artistic values. We have seen that one of P.'s implicit intentions is the redirection of attention from false aesthetic to true, from "bird-poets" to originality. Yet P. also stresses contemporary Rome's critical inability, a Rome which nevertheless awards praise to what it perceives as artistic excellence. At 1.49-53 P. figuratively "shakes out" such misdirected praise, revealing once more the perverse nature of Neronian literary aestheticism:

> nam 'belle' hoc excute totum:
> quid non intus habet? non hic est Ilias Atti
> ebria veratro? non siqua elegidia crudi
> dictarunt proceres? non quidquid denique lectis
> scribitur in citreis?

Praise of artistry is (mis)directed toward the likes of an "Iliad drunk on hellebore" (*Ilias ...lebria veratro*, 50-1), "petty elegies" (*elegidia*, 51), and "whatever is written on citrus

---

[37] This dichotomy between the artistic and the ethic may be, one could argue, essentially false. Yet the issue certainly lends itself to discussion, given the combination in P. and J. both of poetic form and ethical commentary. (For an earlier discussion of this type, see e.g. Sullivan [1968] 106ff., "Petronius: Artist or Moralist?"). On poetic form in general, it is plausible that both P. and J. chose the dactylic hexameter (satiric) format for two positive reasons. First, both cite Lucilius, who indeed standardized this format for Roman satire, as their literary prototype. Second, both parody epic especially; epic (conventionally in dactylic hexameter) is parodied by (innovative) imitation of its meter and form. In the case of P., moreover, the "limping iambic" meter of the *Prologue* has been explained (Ch. 1) as likewise parodic; lame poetry as subject is parodied by formal incorporation of "limping" metrics.

couches" (i.e. by wealthy dabblers, *quidquid denique lectis/scribitur in citreis*, 52-3). It is therefore quite requisite that P. disclaim artistic inspiration; contemporary aesthetics are perverse.

P.'s artistry aims at aesthetic revolution, a rearrangement (even deliberate dissolution) of the conventions of current aestheticism. To understand this is key to understanding the ways in which P.'s poetic artistry is manifested. P. is, in short (paradoxically it may seem), an anti-aesthetic artist. The artistic structure of his verse is most characteristic when it is most originally unorthodox. Some of P.'s most noteworthy poetic constructions are in fact produced by semantic or linguistic misconstructions (this we have seen even as early as the *Prologue*; cf. e.g., *cantare ... Pegaseium nectar*).

While P. employs a language and syntax which may seem to impart, in some instances much more than others, meanings which are indeterminate, we can nevertheless extract from the text of P. given and fixed (invariable) meanings. Yet to do this successfully requires the achievement of a "close" reading of the text, through which we allow P.'s meaning to approach us. It is only then that P.'s carefully architected semantic intent becomes apparent. We must allow ourselves to be mentally manipulated, so to speak, by the text rather than attempting to manipulate the text in an effort to force it into alignment with anything resembling a preconception. For to do this is to risk the text's failure. We must allow the poet to be a poet, let the verses direct us to that level of (conscious) perception intended by their creator. This is how music is best appreciated; we do not, generally, listen to music with a preconception of its purpose and/or direction in mind. It is possible, when hearing music, even for the first time, to be at once both passive and attentive, and so should we be in respect to P.'s "music" as well. We must also "listen" to this "music" in its entirety, perceiving all its aspects simultaneously, for only then can we appreciate the interrelationships of these aspects -- interrelationships which essentially dictate the final nature (and reveal the original nature) of the composition (but not necessarily our perception of it).

P. most certainly displays a consistent aesthetic consciousness. Yet P.'s discourse exhibits a compositional form which consistently strives for unconformity--unconformity in respect to the general composition of his contemporaries. If poetic form reflects its intent, and P.'s poetic intent involves precisely the dissolution of (common) poetic value-assumptions, then P.'s poetic form will necessarily appear dissolute.[38] Formal aspects of P.'s poetic construct (ironically, it may seem) reveal consistently design at unconformity.

For example, the Stoic imagery of causticity (e.g., *mordaci ... aceto*, 5.86) which helps to advance P.'s dichotomy of philosophical freedom and slavery, reflects P.'s literary philosophy. P.'s interlocutors are often self-dissolving, speaking as they do in calculated opposition to P.'s voices of literary/philosophical didacticism. Yet in P.'s picture of Neronian (literary) society, hypocrisy is expected. Recall for example 1.55-7:

> et "verum" inquis "amo, verum mihi dicite de me."
> qui pote? vis dicam? nugaris, cum tibi, calve,
> pinguis aqualiculus propenso sesquipede extet.

There is a catalytic play here on the interlocutor's expectation of praise--praise which would be insincere, but nevertheless expected (*qui pote? vis dicam?*). P.'s "lover of truth" in fact has no conception of the truth, or at least is so conditioned to hypocrisy that he does not expect to hear it; presumably he would not request it otherwise. The impact of P.'s response to the interlocutor is delayed. "How's it possible [to tell you the truth about yourself]" (*qui pote?*) suggests the meaning: "It is impossible ...." Yet the satirist's answer is the sudden, formally unexpected and caustic: *nugaris, cum tibi, calve* ...; the

---

[38] Form and style are in P. especially tied to his satiric (quarrelsome) stance, which is of course highly literary in nature. Thus the "artistry" of P.'s composition is a response to the "artistic poetry" which he attacks. Again, P.'s experimentally forceful verbal combinations are *per se* protest against poetic convention (with which P. is as much concerned as with the general moral corruption of society).

(offensive) truth is actually revealed, and the regular (albeit perverse and hypocritical) format of (patron/client) flattery is dissolved.[39]

P. actually plays (self-consciously) off his own abrupt style in many instances by means of a formulaic questioning of this abruptness (often presented by an interlocutor). Thus P. not only admits his abrupt style, but also anticipates a (typical) reaction to it.[40] This is a significant interrelationship between form and meaning. Likewise, P.'s definition of context is frequently no more than parenthetical, brief lip-service to the satiric convention of providing a (dramatic) context. In the opening lines of two satires, for example,[41] dialogue actually precedes any definition of context; the style is deliberately forceful and sudden. This format of post-positive, parenthetical introduction of context assists meaning precisely because it suggests that context can be relatively unimportant for the conveyance of the satiric message, or meaning itself. *Unus ait comitum*, 3.7, is both vague and parenthetical. And it is indeed unnecessary to comprehend a specific context for this drama in order to appreciate the satire's commentary on wasted youth, sloth, and lack of philosophical conscientiousness. This *comes* whom we are to imagine proves universally significant precisely by his indefinition; he could exist in virtually any context (even the metaphysical or psychic) for anyone.

---

[39] P.'s calculated rejection of the hypocritical tradition is suggested also notably at 1.8: "Who doesn't -- ah, if [only] it were right to speak -- but it is right ...," (*quis non -- ah, si fas dicere -- sed fas*). *Quis non ... is* recalled again not until 1.121, providing a relationship between the beginning and the end of P.'s program: *auriculas asini quis non habet?* Note too the relationship between 1.2 ("*quis leget haec?*" "*min tu istud ais? nemo hercule.*") and 1.134 (the last line of *Sat.* 1): *his mane edictum, post prandia Calliroen do.* The *his* referred to at 1.134 relates (as well as to those types described at vv. 1.127-33) to all those excluded from P.'s readership by the *nemo* of v. 1.2.

[40] Cf. e.g., the response presented (by the interlocutor) to P. 5.1-4 (*vatibus hic mos est ...*): "Where are you going with these [statements]?" ("*quorsum haec ...*").

[41] I.e. P. 3.1-7; 4.1-3.

Similarly, to consider the example of *Satire* 4, the accusative question, *rem populi tractas?*, 4.1, precedes its context. Since the question takes precedence over context, it possesses more power, so to speak. Forceful indignation is thereby strengthened. The introduction of Socrates is literally parenthetical, interrupting as it does Socrates' opening address to Alcibiades:

> "Rem populi tractas?" barbatum haec crede magistrum
> dicere, sorbitio tollit quem dira cicutae.
> "quo fretus? dic hoc, magni pupille Pericli." (4.1-3)

As has been asserted,[42] the attack on Alcibiades by Socrates is not so specific as its context would ostensibly suggest. The messages imparted here are in fact universally applicable. The format of the (Socratic) dialogue relates to the satiric message most clearly, perhaps, in that it presents an opportunity for the satirist's victim to defend himself against (Stoic) sarcasm--the defense naturally fails, and Socrates as satirist thus emerges with his message confirmed. The Roman (Neronian) context into which this Socratic dialogue is interwoven itself affirms the universal (not to mention timeless) nature of the philosophical admonition: *respue quod non es ... tecum habita*, 4.51, 52.

Imagery too is an important formal aspect. We have seen that P. uses the persona of a "Socratic satirist" to convey his philosophical message in *Satire* 4. Yet the dualistic form of the mock dialogue assists the development of the satire's (philosophical) meaning also in that images are created which are likewise dualistic; we have a kind of dialogue between images. These underlying images in fact depend on the dualistic form, complement, and define it. These two (formal) images are dilation and reduction. Dilation is embodied by Alcibiades; reduction of the Alcibiades figure (and of those of whom he is typical) is the accomplishment of the "Socratic satirist."

---

[42] See p. 49 n. 23.

Yet the basically antithetical images (of dilation and reduction) are amplified, so to speak, by references to "greasiness" and "wound," "spitting out" and "truncation." Note first the development of the dilation of the Alcibiades prototype: "to have lived with greased platter" (*uncta vixisse patella*, 17); "puff up" (*suffla*, 20); "idle greased" (*unctus cesses*, 33); "you've a blind wound" (*caecum vulnus habes*, 44). This prototype is "reduced" throughout the satiric dialogue, yet its most pointed reduction is realized in the satire's final lines: "Spit out what you're not" (*respue quod non es*, 51); "You'll realize how truncated your furnishings are" (*noris quam sit tibi curta supellex*, 52).

P. 4 is thus an aesthetic experiment--an experiment with dialogue and persona, in which both format and voice are mutated, combined, meshed into a poetic hybrid. The aesthetic aspects of P.4 strike one as rather more remarkable than the ethical aspects, especially given the fact that, as *topos*, lack of philosophical consciousness is by no means unique to *Satire* 4. Further, P.'s poetry conveys what might be aptly termed an aesthetic ethic, or ethic of aesthetics. For P. ethics and aesthetics are indeed inextricably bound together; P. consistently presents the contemporary (Neronian) literary aesthetic as reflective of contemporary ethics. Aestheticism has lost its (former) ethical foundations. P.'s Neronian representatives of both literature and society display, as we have seen, especially signs of emasculation, nervelessness, and pretension.

In conclusion, it might be well to consider once again the concise description of P.'s character voiced ostensibly by Cornutus at 5. 14-16:
> verba togae sequeris iunctura callidus acri,
> ore teres modico, pallentis radere mores
> doctus et ingenuo culpam defigere ludo.

It would seem, at first glance perhaps, that there is equal emphasis in the above lines on poetic artistry and moral potency. P. chooses the appropriate words, combines them in skillful juxtaposition, and maintains modest discourse. Likewise, "learned" (*doctus*), he can "scrape" (*radere*) pallid habits and mark fault for censorship. Yet to censure fault and to criticize bad habits are essentially, of course, the same thing. P.'s morality therefore, as referred to here, is quite one-dimensional. His artistry, however, involves several aspects. Choice of diction, how that diction is employed, and tone of discourse, while interrelated aspects, are nevertheless distinct. Further, note the final word of Cornutus' description. The adjective *ingenuo*, with its range of meanings, is set up early in the last line so as to create anticipation of the noun it modifies. The climax of Cornutus' description, and clarification of *ingenuo* as well, derive from *ludo*. P. certainly censures fault, yet he does so, importantly, *ingenuo ludo*, by means of freeborn amusement. This is a reference to P.'s artistry; doctor of morality, P. is freely, and by nature, satiric artist.

3a. Interrelationships of Form, Style and Meaning in Juvenal

It is certainly valid to assert that, in comparison to P., J. tends towards a formal compositional style which can be described as rhetorical. We have observed, for example, J.'s rhetorical questions at the very beginning of his program:

> Semper ego auditor tantum? numquamne reponam
> vexatus totiens rauci Theseide Cordi?
> impune ergo mihi recitaverit ille togatas,
> hic elegos? impune diem consumpserit ingens
> Telephus aut summi plena iam margine libri
> scriptus et in tergo necdum finitus Orestes? (1.1-6)

Forceful language and the force of rhetorical repetition creates an almost litigious tone which helps to define J.'s indignant stance. Like P., J. too ensures immediately his disassociation from contemporary *litterati*. The overwhelming body poetic which so irritates J. is itself described in overwhelming detail: *Theseide*, 2; *togatas*, 3; *elegos*,4; *ingens/Telephus*, 4-5; *Orestes*, 6 (this *Orestes* is over-long, and so is its description).

We have also seen that the diverse *farrago* of topics introduced by J. in *Satire* 1 (*quidquid agunt homines*, 85 [if retained and not deleted]) is presented in a form which is itself "patchwork." Form and subject are directly reflective of one another. This, in combination with rhetorical interrogation, causes the reader to supply his own answers-- answers to questions which are calculated to lead us toward sympathy with the message imparted. Consider the example of 1.30-31:

> nam quis iniquae
> tam patiens urbis, tam ferreus, ut teneat se [?]

We as readers must agree (or at least sympathize) with J.'s message, else we would admit our own "ironness." By 1.45, J. has developed his rhetorical stylistic form to the point where he can incorporate a *praeteritio*: "Why should I [even bother] to mention with what rage my dry liver burns ...?" (*quid referam quanta siccum iecur ardeat ira*, 45). Thus we can say that J.'s form of composition is, in a rhetorical sense at least, closer to the traditional poetic norms of his period; aesthetic experimentation of the Persian type is eschewed in favor of more directly indignant expression. J.'s method of presentation of socio-ethical commentary (criticism) does not involve, as does that of P., the implied dissolution of societal values by the deliberate and calculated dissolution of poetic convention. Yet in order to address the question of J. as aestheticist or ethicist, it is best to base discussion on illustration. Considered below is J. 10, a compositional specimen replete with commentary on moral issues and likewise formally conspicuous.

(Arguably perhaps) *Satire* 10 is J.'s most ethically oriented. It will provide a suitable model therefore for an investigation of the question at hand: is its emphasis primarily moral/ethical/religious, or are these apparent concerns rather incidental to a predominant attention to aesthetic expression?

The moral/ethical/religious exhortations of the piece are not difficult to isolate. Wealth, eloquence and fame, longevity, beauty (for one's children), wife and offspring are all the desiderata of the ethically blind.[43] Similarly, J. makes a suggestion, more brief by far than his exposition of false ethics, as to what are the proper desiderata--desiderata which cultivate virtue and lead to the tranquil life (*semita certe/tranquillae per virtutem patet unica vitae*, 363-4):

> orandum est ut sit mens sana in corpore sano.
> fortem posce animum mortis terrore carentem,
> qui spatium vitae extremum inter munera ponat
> naturae, qui ferre queat quoscumque labores,
> nesciat irasci, cupiat nihil et potiores
> Herculis aerumnas credat saevosque labores
> et venere et cenis et pluma Sardanapalli. (10. 356-362)

---

[43] E.g. as desiderata of the ethically misguided: wealth (*crescant ut opes*, 24); eloquence and fame (*Eloquiam ac famam ... /optare*, 114-15); longevity ("*Da spatium vitae, multos da, Iuppiter, annos*," 188); beauty for one's children (*Formam optat modico pueris, maiore puellis/murmure*, 289-90); wife and offspring (*coniugium petimus partumque uxoris*, 352). Further, the ethics of the "mob" (*turba Remi*, 73) are inconsistent and situational, although appetite for "bread and games" remains constant (*sequitur fortunam*, 73; *anxius optat,/panem et circenses*, 80-1).

This then is the sum of J.'s ideal ethic, an ethic which seems a direct call for Stoic durability, but recalls even more the traditional Epicurean perspective.[44]

But what of the aesthetic concerns J. displays in *Satire* 10? Significantly, on a general level, narrative technique and 'personal' tone here signal a new experiment by J.[45] What this experiment entails is essentially an adaptation (facilitated by both persona and poetic format), and the aesthetics of the satire reside largely in the way this adaptation is realized and finally manifested. Specifically, what J. accomplishes is the adaptation to satire of the concept of the moral treatise (just as he adapts the concept of the consolatory epistle in *Satire* 12); an adaptation such as this of course implies artistic exercise.

Again, there is little, if anything, in J. 10 which is new-fashioned from an ethical standpoint.[46] What is unique and artistically remarkable about J. 10 is its literary development--development of form, specific examples to support propositions, and (even in respect to J.'s other satires) the persona through which the piece is presented.

Common ethical beliefs are introduced systematically throughout *Satire* 10 by a moralistic persona and systematically disproved. Introductory references to truth (*vera bona*, 3), error and reason (*erroris nebula, ratione*, 4), and divine providence (*di faciles*, 8), establish the satire's tone early. Yet this suggestion of philosophy, ethics and religion,

---

[44] Cf. Ferguson (1979) 254: "J.'s aim is a peaceful life (*tranquillae ... vitae* 10, 364), and this, the statement that you cannot achieve it except through virtue, came straight from Epicurus. The whole analysis is Epicurean ...."

[45] Braund (1988) 184-5, for example, sees *Sat.* 10 as marking the adoption by J. of an [experimentally] different persona from those of *Sats.* 1-9: "Book IV, Satires 10-12, presents us with a new *persona*, related to that of Book III but different." Braund defines this new persona as Democritean, the structure of *Sat.* 10 "more clearly established ... than any of Juvenal's earlier poems." Specifically, the structure, asserts Braund, is like that of Horace's "so-called diatribe satires, *Serm.* 1.1-3." Cf. also Ferguson (1979) 254: "The poem is more clearly structured than any of the other satires." For a schematic breakdown of *Sat.* 10's structural segments, see Ferguson 254. Yet the poem is (aesthetically and ethically) not simply a Horatian diatribe voiced by a Democritean persona.

[46] Cf. Ferguson (1979) 275: "The whole collection of true prayers is derived from the commonplaces of Hellenistic philosophy: we may see something similar in Cic. *Tusc. Disp.* 5. See also Martial 10, 47." Likewise, re. *mens sana in corpore sano*, 356, "J's most familiar epigram ... is in fact a variant of a stock prayer ...".

while serving to introduce (accurately) the type of subject-matter around which the poem will evolve, just as importantly sets up J.'s artistic foundation.

The preliminary form of the satire is essentially this: the themes of philosophy, ethics and religion are established by way of introduction; three examples of ethical self-victimization are introduced as prelude to the theme of wealth versus modesty (v. 15; Longinus, Seneca and the Lateranii, all wealthy sufferers under Nero, are contrasted unfavorably with one who owns nothing [*vacuus ... viator*, 22]); this theme of wealth as inferior to modesty leads to a discussion of extravagance (even official, exemplified by *praetextae, trabeae, fasces, lectica, tribunal*, etc., 35ff.), and it is here that the persona adopts whatever Democritean aspects we imagine it to display;[47] Heraclitus is humorously dismissed (*mirandum est unde ille oculis suffecerit umor*, 32), and Democritus is (humorously) acknowledged as a "great man" (*summos ... viros*, 49) with an admirable immunity to Fortune (*manderet laqueum mediumque ostenderet unguem*, 53); finally, verses 54-5 mark the beginning of the main body of the satire, with its elaborate examples of misdirected ethics:

> ergo supervacua aut quae perniciosa petuntur?
> propter quae fas est genua incerare deorum?

The nature of these misdirected ethics, or desiderata, has been outlined (cf. above). As was asserted, these are simple, even commonplace. Yet the aesthetic value of J. 10 lies notably in the exposition and manner of example-oriented description of these ethically perverse commonplaces. Consider a portion of J.'s first topical description, that which deals with public honor:

> iam strident ignes, iam follibus atque caminis
> ardet adoratum populo caput et crepat ingens
> Seianus, deinde ex facie toto orbe secunda

---

[47] My view is that, while the narrator (persona) certainly does seem to approve of the Democritean outlook on life, he does not clearly maintain what we can demonstrate to be a Democritean persona after v. 54 (cf. n45). *Ergo*, 54, in fact marks a turning away from Democritus and a renewed attention to misguided prayer.

fiunt urceoli, pelves, sartago, matellae. (10. 61-64)

Iam ... iam (61) facilitates a vivid vignette wherein "from the face second in the whole world" (63) are made "jugs, basins, a frying-pan, piss-pots" (64). A "publicly adored personage" (*adoratum populo caput*, 62) is transformed into a piss-pot; the image is profound, its verbal conveyance artistically striking.

The futility of "eloquence and fame" (*eloquium ac famam*, 114) is stressed first with reference to two of history's most famously eloquent, Demosthenes and Cicero. Both of course suffered for their outspokenness; yet Cicero, had he remained an artist (poet), however uninspired and vainglorious, would have avoided the "swords of Antony" (*Antoni gladios*, 123). Both the artistic inability and personal conceit of a Cicero are parodied by J.:

"o fortunatam natam me consule Romam:" (10.122)

While the above verse offsets the gravity of Cicero's death-description (vv. 120-21), it is included by J. purely for aesthetic impact.[48]

It is too purely for aesthetic amusement that J. describes the number of illnesses (*morborum omne genus*, 219) to which the geriatric falls prey. In the description (vv. 220-26) there are incidental stabs at various characters, none of whom is especially significant. Again, it is the humor and artistry of the passage that impresses, not the moral import:

> morborum omne genus, quorum si nomina quaeras,
> promptius expediam quot amaverit Oppia moechos,
> quot Themison aegros autumno occiderit uno,
> quot Basilus socios, quot circumscripserit Hirrus
> pupillos, quot longa viros exorbeat uno
> Maura die, quot discipulos inclinet Hamillus;
> percurram citius quot villas possideat nunc
> quo tondente gravis iuveni mihi barba sonabat.

---

[48] Parody of poesy is of course, as especially evident in P., itself an art. Note J.'s alliteration to parody that of Cicero's line at 10. 123-4: ... *si sic/ omnia dixisset*.

Basically, the above lines betray J.'s 'postclassical' reaction to conventional techniques of poetic description (in this case the technique of decorative periphrasis); yet this type of aesthetic is adapted to a subject matter which is obscene and unethical. Thus J. proves that he can compose artistically, yet what he is compelled to describe is not lofty, graceful or beautiful (socially irrelevant), but rather inelegant and squalid (socially relevant).

The aesthetics, therefore, of J. (as here exemplified by *Satire* 10) involve notably the adaptation of what might be called 'classical' poetic formalities (techniques) to poetry which describes (through a persona which certainly appears at times moralistic) the ugly and the absurd. This is quite different from P.'s method, whose 'post-classicism' is manifested more in mutation of conventional diction and syntax. J. tends to retain 'classical' form and technique, yet he uses them in connection with a subject matter which, in combination with this form and technique, forms what is a totally unorthodox final product. This is how J. causes his reader to react, to acknowledge that his poetry contains, even on a formal level, a statement against literature which retains established form yet eschews relevancy.

BIBLIOGRAPHY

Abel, K. (1986) "Die dritte Satire des Persius als dichterische Kuntswerk" in *Kontinuität und Wandel. Lateinische Poesie von Naevius bis Baudelaire. Festschrift Franco Munari* (edd. Stache, U. J., Maaz, W. & Wagner, F.) 151 Hildesheim

Adamietz, J. (1972) *Untersuchungen zu Juvenal. Hermes Einzelsch.* 26

Adams, J. N. (1982) *The Latin Sexual Vocabulary*, London

Ahl, F. (1984) "The art of safe criticism in Greece and Rome," *AJP* 105: 174-208

Alexander, W. H. (1947) "Juvenal 7.126-128," *CP* 42: 123-4

Allen, C. A. & Stephens, G. D. (1962) *Satire: Theory and Practice*, Belmont (California)

Anderson, W. S. (1988) "Juvenal Satire 15: Cannibals and Culture" in *The Imperial Muse: Ramus Essays on Roman Literature of the Empire* (ed. Boyle, A. J.), Berwick

----- (1982) *Essays on Roman Satire*, New Jersey

----- (1981-2) "Recent work in Roman satire (1968-1978)," *CW* 75: 273-99

----- (1958) "Persius 1.107-110," *CQ* 52.8: 195ff.

----- (1955) "Juvenal. Evidence on the years A.D. 117-128," *CP* 50: 255-7

Arnold, E. V. (1911) *Roman Stoicism*, Cambridge

Austin, F. M. (1903) "Cacophony in Juvenal, Horace and Persius," *AJP* 24: 452-5

Barbu, N. I. (1961) "Remarques sur le style poétique de Juvénal," *StudClas* 3: 345-53

Bardon, H. (1975a) "Perse et la réalité des choses," *Latomus* 34: 319ff.

----- (1975b) "A Propos de Perse: surréalisme et collage," *Latomus* 34: 675-98

----- (1976) "A Propos de Perse: Morale et Satire," *RCCM* 18: 49-70

Barr, W. (1981) "'Res' = 'a thing'? Persius 4.1," *PLLS* 3 (Arca 7): 4222-3

Beaujeu, J. (1966) "La réligion de Juvénal" in *Mélanges offerts a Jérome Carcopino*:71-81 Paris

Beikircher, H. (1969) *Kommentar zur VI des A. Persius Flaccus*, Wien, Köln, Graz

Bellandi, F. (1973) "Poetica dell' *indignatio* e sublime satirico in Giovenale," *ASNP* 3: 53-94

----- (1974) "Naevolus Cliens," *Maia* 26: 279-99

----- (1974-5) "Giovenale e la degrazione della clienta (interpretazione della sat. VII)" *DArch* 8: 384-437

----- (1980) *Etica diatribica e protesta sociale nelle satire di Giovenale*, Bologna

Berkowitz, L. & Brunner, T. F. (1967) *Index Verborum Quae In Saturis Auli Persi Flacci Reperiuntur*, Hildesheim

Bishop, J. D. (1976) "Juvenal 9.96, a parody?," *Latomus* 35: 597

Bloom, E. A. & L. D. (1979) *Satire's Persuasive Voice*, Cornell U. P.

Bo, D. (1969) *A. Persi Flacci Saturarum Liber*, Paravia, Torino

----- (1967) *Auli Persii Flacci Lexicon*, Hildesheim

Bodoh, J. J. (1970) "Artistic control in the Satires of Juvenal," *Aevum* 44: 475-82

Bolisani, E. (1962-3) "Persio imitato da Giovenale," *AIV* 121: 367-81

Bonner, S. F. (1969) *Roman declamation in the late Republic and early Empire*, Liverpool

----- (1977) *Roman education*, London

Bouet, P. L. C. et al. (1978) *Konkordanz zu den Satiren des Persius Flaccus*, Hildesheim, New York

Boyle, A. J. (1986) *The Chaonian Dove: Studies in the Eclogues, Georgics, and Aeneid of Virgil*, Leiden

----- (ed.) (1988) *The Imperial Muse: To Juvenal Through Ovid: Ramus Essays on Roman Literature of the Empire*, Berwick

Bramble, J. C. (1974) *Persius and the Programmatic Satire: A Study In Form and Imagery*, Cambridge

Braund, S. H. (1981) "Juvenal 8.58-9," *CQ* 31: 221-3

----- (1982) "Juvenal 7.50-52," *Phoenix* 36: 162-6

----- (1988) *Beyond Anger: A study of Juvenal's third Book of Satires*, Cambridge

Braund, S. H. & Cloud, J. D. (1981) "Juvenal: a diptych," *LCM* 6: 195-208

----- (1983) "Juvenal's traducement again (2.153-163)," *LCM* 8: 50-1

Brind'amour, L. & P. (1971) "La deuxieme satire de Perse," *Latomus* 30: 999ff.

Brown, P. (1988) *The Body and Society, Men, Women and Sexual Renunciation in Early Christianity*, Columbia

Brown, P. G. McC. (1972) "Two passages in Juvenal's eighth Satire," *CQ* 22: 374-5

Brugnoli, G. (1968) "Il Dialogus e Giovenale," *RCCM* 10: 252-9

Brunner, T. F. (1971) "A note on Persius 5.134ff.," *CQ* 21: 487

Buecheler, F. (1886) "Der Text des Persius," *RhM* 41: 454ff.

Burriss, E. E. (1926) "The Religious Element in the Satires of Juvenal," CW 20: 19-21

Buscaroli, P. (1924) *Persio studiato in rapporto a Orazio e Giovenale*

Cebe, J-P. (1966) *La caricature et la parodie dans le monde romain antique des origines a Juvénal*, Paris

Clarke, M. L. (1968) "Juvenal 7.150-153," *CP* 63: 295-6

----- (1973) "Juvenal 7.242-243," *CR* 23: 12

Clausen, W. V. (1956) *A. Persi Flacci Saturarum Liber*, Oxford

----- (1959, repr. 1977) *A. Persi Flacci et D. Iuni Iuvenalis Saturae*, Oxford

Clay, D. (1983) *Lucretius and Epicurus*

Cloud, J. D. & Braund, S. H. (1982) "Juvenal's libellus - a farrago?," *G & R* 29: 77-85

Coffey, M. (1976) *Roman Satire*, London, New York

Collinge, N. E. (1967) "A conversation in Persius," *CR* 17: 132

Colton, R. E. (1963) "Juvenal and Martial on literary and professional men," *CB* 39: 49-52

----- (1966) "Juvenal and Martial on the equestrian order," *CJ* 61: 157-9

----- (1966) "Juvenal on recitations," *CB* 42: 81-5

Conches, G. de (1980) *Glossae In Iuvenalem* (ed. Wilson, B.) Paris

Conington, J. (1893) *The Satires of A. Persius Flaccus*, Oxford

Connor, P. (1988) "The Satires of Persius: A Stretch of the Imagination" (in Boyle 1988)

Consoli, S. (1921) "La satira 9 di Giovenale nella tradizione della cultura sino alla fine del medio evo," *RFIC* 49: 79-97

Courtney, E. (1966) "Juvenaliana," *BICS* 13: 38-43

----- (1967) "The transmission of Juvenal's text," *BICS* 14: 38-50

----- (1974) "Some thought-patterns in Juvenal," *Hermathena* 118: 15-21

----- (1975) "The interpolations in Juvenal," *BICS* 22: 147-62

----- (1980) *A Commentary on the Satires of Juvenal*, London

Creekmore, H.(1963) *The Satires of Juvenal*

Crook, J. A. (1967) "A study in decoction," *Latomus* 26: 363-76

Davey, F. (1971) "Juvenal 7.242ff.," *CR* 21: 11

De Decker, J. (1913) *Juvenalis declamans: étude sur la rhétorique déclamatoire dans les Satires de Juvénal*, Ghent

Dessen, C. S. (1968) *Iunctura Callidus Acri: A Study of Persius' Satires*, Urbana, Chicago, London

Dick, B. F. (1969) "Seneca and Juvenal 10," *HSPh* 73: 237-46

Diggle, J. (1974) "Juvenal 8.220," *CR* 24: 183-4

Dubrocard, M. (1967) "Recherches par ordinateur sur la langue et le vocabulaire de Juvénal," résumé in *REL* 45: 37-9

----- (1970) "Quelques remarques sur la distribution et la signification des hapax dans les Satires de Juvénal," *AFLNice* 11: 131-40

----- (1974) "Quelques remarques sur l'utilisation de l'impératif dans les Satires de Juvénal," *AFLNice* 21: 259-69

----- (1976) *Juvénal, Satires. Index verborum relevés statistiques*, Hildesheim

----- (1979) "L'utilisation des catégories grammaticales dans les Satires de Juvénal: essai d'analyse factorielle," *AFLNice* 35: 259-73

Duff, J. D. (1898, repr. 1970) D. *Iunii Iuvenalis Saturae XIV*, Cambridge

Duff, J. W. (1936) *Roman Satire: Its Outlook on Social Life*, Berkeley, London

Dürr, J. (1888) *Das Leben Juvenals*, Ulm

----- (1903) "Juvenal and Hadrian," in *Festschrift zu Otto Hirschfelds* 447-51

Eden, P. T. (1985) "Juvenalia," *Mnemosyne* 38: 334-52

Edmunds, L. (1972) "Juvenal's thirteenth Satire," *RhM* 115: 59-73

Eichholtz, D. E. (1956) "The art of Juvenal and his tenth Satire," *G & R* 3: 61-9

Elliot, R. C. (1960) *The Power of Satire: Magic, Ritual, Art*, Princeton U. P.

Ercole, P. (1931) "Stazio e Giovenale," *RIGI* 15: 43-50

Ferguson, J. (1979) *Juvenal: The Satires*, New York

Fiske, G. C. (1916) "*Udas ante fores*: Persius v. 165-66," *CP* 11: 336-8

----- (1920, repr. 1966) *Lucilius and Horace: A Study in the Classical Theory of Imitation*, Hildesheim

Fletcher, G. B. A. (1944) "Alliteration in Juvenal," *DUJ* 5: 59-64

----- (1976) "Juvenaliana," *Latomus* 35: 108-16

Flintoff, E. (1974) "New light on the early life of Juvenal," *WS* 8: 156-9

----- (1982) "Food for thought. Some imagery in Persius Satire 2," *Hermes* 110: 341ff.

Foucault, M. (1988) *The care of the self. The history of sexuality, Volume 3*

Frassinetti, P. (1955) "Note a Persio e a Giovenale," *RFIC* 33: 405-15

Fredericks, S. C. (1969) *Mos Maiorum in Juvenal and Tacitus* (Diss. Univ. of Pennsylvania)

----- (1971a) "Rhetoric and morality in Juvenal's 8th Satire," *TAPA* 102: 111-32

----- (1971b) "Calvinus in Juvenal's thirteenth Satire," *Arethusa* 4: 219-31

----- (1973) "The function of the Prologue (1-20) in the organisation of Juvenal's third Satire," *Phoenix* 27: 62-7

----- (1976) "Juvenal's fifteenth Satire," *ICS* 1: 174-89

----- (1979) "Irony and overstatement in the Satires of Juvenal," *ICS* 4: 178-91

Friedländer, L. (1895) *D. Iunii Juvenalis Saturarum Libri V*, Leipzig

Frye, N. (1944) "The Nature of Satire," *Univ. of Toronto Quarterly* 14: 75-89

Gauger, F. (1936-7) *Zeitschilderung und Topik bei Juvenal* (Diss. Greifswald)

Gehlen, J. (1881) *De Juvenale Vergilii imatore* (Diss. Erlangen)

Gérard, J. (1964) "Présence de l'histoire dans les Satires de Juvénal," *IL* 16: 103-09, 154-8

----- (1970) "Juvénal et les associations d'artistes grecs a Rome," *REL* 48: 309-31

----- (1976) *Juvénal et la Réalité Contemporaine*, Paris

Giangrande, G. (1965) "Juvenalian emendations and interpretations," *Eranos* 63: 26-41

Goodenough, E. R. (1953-8) *Jewish symbols in the Graeco-Roman period* (8 vols.)

Graur, A. (1962) "Multa contingere virga (Iuvenal VIII.7)," *StudClas* 4: 241-3

Green, P. (1967) *Juvenal: The Sixteen Satires*, Harmondsworth

Griffith, J. G. (1951) "Varia Iuvenaliana," *CR* 1: 138-42

----- (1956) "Author variants in Juvenal. A reconsideration," in *Festschrift Bruno Snell* 101-11

----- (1962) "Juvenal and stage-struck patricians," *Mnemosyne* 15: 256-61

----- (1963) "The survival of the longer of the so-called Oxford fragments of Juvenal's sixth Satire," *Hermes* 91: 104-14

----- (1969a) "Frustrula Iuvenaliana," *CQ* 19: 379-87

----- (1969b) "Juvenal, Statius and the Flavian establishment," *G & R* 16: 134-50

----- (1970) "The ending of Juvenal's first Satire and Lucilius, Book 30," *Hermes* 98: 56-72

Gundel, W. & H. G. (1966) *Astrologumena: Die astrologische Literatur in der Antike und ihre Geschichte*

Halkin, L. (1932) "Sexta quaque die, *Sat.* 7.160," *LEC* 117-23

Halliday, W. R. (1924) "Persius ii. 37," *CR* 38: 169

Hanssen, J. S. Th. (1951) *Latin Diminutives: A Semantic Study*

Hardy, E. G. (1893) "Juv. Sat. viii.247," *CR* 7: 23

Harrison, E. L. (1960) "Neglected hyperbole in Juvenal," *CR* 10: 99-101

Hartmann, A. (1908) *De Inventione Iuvenalis*, Basel

Harvey, R. A. (1981) *A Commentary on Persius*, Leiden

Heilmann, W. (1967) "Zur Kompositionder vierten Satire und des ersten Satirenbuches Juvenals," *RhM* 110: 358-70

Heindl, K. (1951) *Bilder, Vergleiche und Beschreibungen bei Juvenal*

Heinrich, C. F. (1839) *Iunii Iuvenalis Satirae*

Hellegouarc'h, J. (1969) "La ponctuation bucolique dans les satires de Juvénal. Etude métrique et stylistique," in *Mélanges René Fohalle* 173-89

----- (1971) "Les idées politiques et l'appartenance sociale de Juvénal," in *Studi in Onore di Eduardo Volterra* 2: 233-45

Helmbold, W. C. (1951) "The structure of Juvenal 1," *UCPCP* 14: 47-60

----- (1956) "Juvenal's twelfth Satire," *CP* 51: 14-23

Helmbold, W. C. & O'Neil, E. N. (1956) "The structure of Juvenal 4," *AJP* 77: 68-73

----- (1959) "The form and purpose of Juvenal's seventh satire," *CP* 54: 100-8

Henderson, J. H. (1989) "Persius' Didactic Satire: the Pupil as Teacher" (unpubl.)

Hendrickson, G. L. (1928a) "The first satire of Persius," *CP* 23: 97-112

----- (1928b) "The third satire of Persius," *CP* 23: 332-42

Henss, D. (1954) "Ist das Lucilius fragment 9 Marx echt?," *Philologus* 98: 159-61.

----- (1955) "Die Imitationstechnik des Persius," *Philologus* 99: 277-94

Hermann, K. F. (1842) *Lectiones Persianae* (3 vols.), Marburg, Leipzig

Highet, G. (1949) "The philosophy of Juvenal," *TAPA* 80: 254-70

----- (1951a) "Juvenal's Bookcase," *AJP* 72: 369-94

----- (1951b) "Sound-effects in Juvenal's poetry," *SPh* 48: 697-706

----- (1952) "Notes on Juvenal," *CR* 2: 70-1

----- (1961) *Juvenal the Satirist: A Study*, Oxford

----- (1962) *The Anatomy of Satire*, Princeton

----- (1974) "Masks and faces in satire," *Hermes* 102: 321-37

Hodgart, M. (1969) *Satire*, London

Hooley, D. M. (1984) "*Mutatis Mutandis*: Imitations of Horace in Persius' First Satire," *Arethusa* 17: 83ff.

----- (1991) "A Vexed Passage in Persius (6.51-52)," *CJ* 87: 13-24

Housman, A. E. (1972) *The Classical Papers of A. E. Housman* (J. Diggle & F. R. D. Goodyear, eds.), London

----- (1931) *D. Iunii Iuuenalis* (2nd edn.), Cambridge

Humphries, R. (1958) *The Satires of Juvenal*, Bloomington

Iorillo, R. J. (1973) "A Juvenalian twit?," *CW* 67: 177

Jachmann, G. (1943) "Studien zu Juvenal," *NAWG* 6: 187-266

Jacoby, F. (1959) "Zwei Doppelfassungen im Juvenaltext," *Hermes* 87: 449-62

Jahn, O. (1851) *D. Iunii Iuvenalis Saturarum Libri V* (rev. F. Bücheler, 1893)

Jackson, R. (1988) *Doctors and Diseases in the Roman Empire* (British Museum Publ.)

Jefferis, J. D. (1939) "Juvenal and Religion," *CJ* 34: 229-33

Jenkinson, J. R. (1973) "Interpretations of Persius' satires 3 and 4," *Latomus* 32: 521-49

----- (1980) *Persius: The Satires*, Warminster

Jensen, B. Frueland (1981-2) "Crime, vice and retribution in Juvenal's Satires," *C & M* 33: 155-68

Jessen, J. (1889) "Witz und Humor im Juvenal," *Phil* 1: 320-7

----- (1900) "Zu Juvenal," *Phil* 13: 505-20

Johnson, R. R. (1973) "Bicolor membrana," *CQ* 23: 339-42

Jones, C. P. (1972) "Juvenal 8.220," *CR* 22: 313

Jones, F. (1982) "A note on Juvenal *Sat.* 7.86," *CQ* 76: 478-9

----- (1983) "Towards an interpretation of Juvenal Satire 11," *AClass* 26: 104-7

Kappelmacher, A. (1903) "Studia Iuvenaliana," *Dissertationes Philologicae Vindobonenses* 7: 159-99

Kelling, L. & Suskin, A. (1951) *Index Verborum Iuvenalis*, Chapel Hill

Kenney, E. J. (1962) "The first Satire of Juvenal," *PCPhS* 8: 29-40

----- (1963) "Juvenal, satirist or rhetorician?," *Latomus* 22: 704-20

----- (1982) & Clausen, W. V. (eds.) *The Cambridge History of Classical Literature* (Vol. 2), Cambridge

Kernan, A. (1965) *The Plot of Satire*, New Haven

Killeen, J. F. (1969) "Juvenal 7.126ff.," *Glotta* 67: 265-6

Kilpatrick, R. S. (1973) "Juvenal's patchwork satires, 4 and 7," *YCIS* 23: 229-41

Knapp, C. (1924) "Juvenal 7.150-168. Ancient oratory," *CW* 18: 65-8

Knoche, U. (1940) *Handschriftliche Grundlagen des Juvenalstextes, Philologus Suppl.* 33.1

----- (1950) *D. Iunius Iuvenalis: 'Saturae'*, Munich

----- (1971) *Die römische Satire* (trans. 1975), Bloomington

Korzeniewski, D. (ed.) (1970a) *Die römische Satire, Wege der Forschung* 238

----- (1970b) "Die zweite Satire des Persius," *Gymnasium* 77: 199-210

Kosztolányi, D. (1922) *Darker Muses: The Poet Nero* (based on 1990 trans. of Fadiman, C.) Corvina

Krenkel, W. (ed.) (1966) *Römische Satire*, Rostock

----- (1970) *Lucilius: Satiren*, Berlin

Kupersmith, W. (1985) *Roman Satirists in Seventeenth-Century England*, Lincoln, London

Kurfess, A. M. (1956) "Juvenal und die Sibylle," *HJ* 76: 79-83

Labriolle, P. de & Villeneuve, F. (1931) *Juvénal Satires*, Paris

Lackenbacher, H. (1937) "Persius und die Heilkunde," *WS* 55: 130-41

LaFleur, R. A. (1975a) "Amicus and amicitia in Juvenal," *CB* 51: 54-8

----- (1975b) "A footnote to 'New light on the early life of Juvenal,'" *WS* 88: 236

----- (1979) "Amicitia and the unity of Juvenal's first book," *ICS* 4: 158-77

Lavagnini, B. (1947) "Motivi diatribici in Lucrezio e in Giovenale," *Athenaeum* 25: 83-8

Lawall, G. (1958) "Exempla and theme in Juvenal's tenth Satire," *TAPA* 89: 25-31

Leach, E. W. (1975) "Neronian pastoral and the world of power," in A. J. Boyle (ed.), *Ancient Pastoral* 122-48

Lee, G. & Barr, W. (1987) *The Satires of Persius*, Liverpool, New Hampshire

Lelievre, F. J. (1972) "Virgil and Juvenal's third Satire," *Euphrosyne* 5: 457-62

Lemaistre, M. F. (1861) *Ouvres Completes de Juvénal et de Perse Suivies des Fragments de Turnus et de Sulpicia*

Leo, F. (1909) "Doppelfassungen bei Iuvenal," *Hermes* 44: 600-17

----- (1910) "Zum Text des Persius und Iuvenal," *Hermes* 45: 41ff.

Lewis, J. D. (1873) *D. Iunii Iuuenalis Satirae*, London

Lindo, L. I. (1974) "The evolution of Juvenal's later satires," *CP* 69: 17-27

Litchfield, H. W. (1914) "National exempla virtutis in Roman literature," *HSP* 25: 1-71

Luck, G. (1972) "The textual history of Juvenal and the Oxford lines," *HSP* 76: 217-32

McCabe, K. (1986) "'Was Juvenal a structuralist?' A look at anachronisms in literary criticism," *G & R* 33: 78-84

McGann, M. J. (1968) "Juvenal's ninth age (13.28ff.)," *Hermes* 96: 509-14

McKay, A. G. & Shepherd, D. M. (1976) *Roman Satire*, Basingstoke

McKim, R. (1986) "Philosophers and Cannibals: Juvenal's Fifteenth Satire," *Phoenix* 40: 58-71

Macleane, A. J. (1867) *Juvenalis et Persii Satirae*

Mack, M. (1951-2) "The muse of satire," *Yale Review* 41: 80-92

Manning, C. E. (1975) "Acting and Nero's conception of the Principate," *G & R* 22: 164-75

Marache, R. (1961) "La revendication sociale chez Martial et Juvénal," *RCCM* 3: 30-67

----- (1964) "Rhétorique et humour chez Juvénal," in *Hommages a J. Bayet* 474-8

----- (1969a) "Crime et épouvante dans les satires de Juvénal," in *Hommages a M. Renard* I 587-94

----- (1969b) "Un usage particular de ergo chez Juvénal," *GIF* 21:241-3

Marcantoni, J. D. (1938a) "A note on Sat. 7.207," *Mnemosyne* 6: 151

----- (1938b) "A note on the third satire of Persius," *Mnemosyne* 3.6: 152

Marmorale, E. V. (1950) *Giovenale* (2nd edn) Bari

----- (1956) *Persio*

Martin, J. M. K. (1939) "Persius - Poet of the Stoics," *G & R* 8:174

Martyn, J. R. C. (1964) "Juvenal on Latin oratory," *Hermes* 92: 121-3

----- (1969) *Friedländer's Essays on Juvenal* (trans.), Amsterdam

----- (1970) "A new approach to Juvenal's first Satire," *Antichthon* 4: 53-61

----- (1979) "Juvenal's wit," *Grazer Beiträge* 8: 219-38

----- (1980) "Further evidence on Juvenal's Oxford fragments," *Scriptorium* 34: 247-53

Marx, F. C. (1905) *Lucilii Carminum Reliquiae* (repr. 1963), Amsterdam

Mason, H. A. (1963) "Is Juvenal a classic?," in Sullivan (1963) 93-176

Mayor, J. E. B. (1872-8) *Thirteen Satires of Juvenal* (2nd edn.), London

----- (1888) "Notes on Juvenal," *JPhilol* 16: 220-8

----- (1892) "Notes on Juvenal Satire VIII," *JPhilol* 20: 252-93

Merwin, W. S. (1961) *The Satires of Persius*, Bloomington

Miller, J. F. (1986) "Disclaiming Divine Inspiration: A Programmatic Pattern," *WS* 99: 159

Morford, M. (1972) "A note on Juvenal 6.627-661," *CP* 67: 198

----- (1973) "Juvenal's thirteenth Satire," *AJP* 94: 26-36

----- (1977) "Juvenal's fifth Satire," *AJP* 98: 219-45

----- (1984) *Persius*, Boston

Morgan, M. H. (1889) "Notes on Persius," *CR* 3: 10-11

----- (1896) "Notes on Persius," *HSCP* 7: 191-203

Morse, C. J. (1956) "Quid do ut (ne). A bargaining construction in Juvenal and the Senecas," *CR* 6: 196-8

Motto, A. L. & Clarke, J. R. (1965) "Per iter tenebricosum. The mythos of Juvenal 3," *TAPA* 96: 267-76

Mussehl, J. (1919) "Bedeutung und Geschichte des Verbums *cevere*," *Hermes* 54: 387-408

Nadeau, Y. (1983) "Juvenal traduced (Juvenal 2.149-159)," *LCM* 8: 14-16

----- (1985) "Traduction and censors (Juvenal 2.159; 8.17; 7.16; 11.31: Virgil A. 6.697ff.)," *LCM* 10: 44-8

Nicholson, F. W. (1897) "The saliva superstition in classical literature," *HSCP* 8: 23-40

Nisbet, R. G. (1918) "The *festuca* and the *alapa* of manumission," *JRS* 8: 1-14

Nisbet, R. G. M. (1963) "Persius" in Sullivan (1963) 39-71

Norcio, G. (1972) "La professione dell' insegnante nel giudizio di Giovenale," *Annali della Pubbl. istruzione* 18: 478-82

O'Neil, E. N. (1960) "The structure of Juvenal's fourteenth Satire," *CP* 55: 251-3

Orentzel, A. E. (1976) "Juvenal and Statius," *CB* 52: 61-2

Owen, S. G. (1893) "Notes on Juvenal," *CR* 7: 400-3

----- (1905) "On the tunica retiarii," *CR* 19: 358-8

----- (1907) *A. Persi Flacci et D. Iuni Iuuenalis Saturae* (2nd edn.)

Paratore, E. (1973-4) "Note di critica testuale Giovenaliana," *ArchClas* 25-6: 491-501

----- (1985) "Surrealismo e iperrealismo in Persio" in *Hommages a Henry Bardon, Collection Latomus* 187: 277-89 (edd. Renard, M. & Laurens, P.)

Pearson, C. H. & Strong, H. A. D. (1892) *Iunii Iuvenalis Saturae XIII* (2nd edn.)

Pepe, L. (1961) "Questioni adrianee. Giovenale e Adriano," *GIF* 14: 163-73

Perelli, L. (1973) Per una nuova interpretazione di Giovenale 7.228-243," *Maia* 25: 107-12

Peterson, R. G. (1973-4) "The Unknown Self in the Fourth Satire of Persius," *CJ* 68: 208

Potter, F. H. (1934) "Creticus and Camerinus, Juvenal 8.38," *CJ* 30: 41-2

Pryor, A. D. (1961) "An approach to the later Satires of Juvenal," résumé in *BICS* 8: 85

----- (1962) "Juvenal's false consolation," *AUMLA* 18: 167-80

----- (1969) "Juvenal's ridiculum acri fortius," summary in *BICS* 16: 170

Quincey, J. H. (1959) "Juvenal, Satire 8.192-196," *Mnemosyne* 12: 139-40

Radermacher, L. (1904) "Zur siebenten Satire Juvenals," *RhM* 59: 525-31

Ramage, E. S. (1978) "Juvenal, Satire 12: on friendship true and false," *ICS* 3: 221-37

----- (1979) "Method and Structure in the Satires of Persius," *ICS* 4: 136

Ramage, E. S., Sigsbee, D. L. & Fredericks, S. C. (1974) *Roman Satirists and their Satire*, Park Ridge (New Jersey)

Ramsay, G. G. (1918) *Juvenal and Persius*, Cambridge (Massachusetts), London

Rankin, H. D. (1969) "Eating People is Right: Petronius 141 and a Topos," *Hermes* 97

Reckford, K. J. (1962) "Studies in Persius," *Hermes* 90: 476-504

Reekmans, T. (1971) "Juvenal's views on social change," *AncSoc* 2: 117-61

Reeve, M. D. (1973) "Gladiators in Juvenal's sixth Satire," *CR* 23: 124-5

----- (1983) "Commentaries on Juvenal," *CR* 33: 27-34

Richards, L. (1966) "Juvénal et les galles de Cybele," *RHR* 169: 51-67

Richlin, A. (1983) *The Garden of Priapus. Sexuality and Aggression in Roman Humor*, New Haven

Richter, W. (1965) "Varia Persiana," *WS* 78: 139ff.

Rist, J. (1969) *Stoic philosophy*

Robertson, D. S. (1928) "Juvenal 8.241," *CR* 42: 60-1

Robinson, S. (1983) *Juvenal: Sixteen Satires Upon The Ancient Harlot*, Manchester

Romano, A. C. (1979) *Irony in Juvenal*, Hildesheim, New York

Rooy, C. A. Van (1965) *Studies in Classical Satire and Related Literary Theory*, Leiden

Rose, H. J. (1924) "Some traps in Persius' first satire," *CR* 38: 63-4

Rudd, N. (1970) "Persiana," *CR* 20: 282-8

----- (1976) *Lines of Enquiry: Studies in Latin Poetry*, London, New York, Melbourne

----- (1979) *The Satires of Horace and Persius, a verse translation with introduction and notes*

----- (1982) "Persius," in Kenney & Clausen (1982) 503-10

----- (1983) "On being traduced (Juvenal 2.149-59)," *LCM* 8: 30

----- (1986) *Themes in Roman Satire*, London

Ruperti, G. A. (1825) *D. Junii Juvenalis Aquinatis Satirae XVI*

Ruyt, F. De (1944) "Quantum in Leucade (Sat. 8.241)," *RBPh* 23: 246-50

Saccone, M. S. (1985) "La Poesia di Persio alla luce degli studi piu recenti (1964-83)" *ANRW* II 32.3 1783f.

Saint-Denis, E. De (1952) "L'humour de Juvénal," *IL* 4: 8-14

Saller, R. P. (1983) "The meaning of faenus in Juvenal's ninth Satire," *PHPhS* 29: 72-6

Sandbach, F. H. (1975) *The Stoics*

Sandford, P. (1890) "Persius *S.* 1.78," *CR* 4: 272

Schmid, P. (1964) "Juvénal. Essai d'une définition stylistique," résumé in *REL* 42: 57-9

Schütze, R. (1904-5) *Juvenalis Ethicus*, Diss. Griefswald

Schulz, W. (1886) "Quaestiones Iuvenalianae," *Hermes* 21: 179-92

Scivoletto, N. (1957) "Plinio il Giovano e Giovenale," *GIF* 10: 133-46

----- (1963) "Presenza di Persio in Giovenale," *GIF* 16: 60-72

Scott, I. G. (1927) *The Grand Style in the Satires of Juvenal* (Smith College Classical Studies 8) Northampton (Massachusetts)

Seager, R. (1977) "Amicitia in Tacitus and Juvenal," *AJAH* 2: 40-50

Serafini, A. (1957) *Studio sulla Satira di Giovenale*, Florence

Settis, S. (1970) "Qui multas facies pingit cito (Iuven. 9.146)," *A & R* 15: 117-21

Shaw, B. D. (1985) "The Divine Economy: Stoicism as Ideology," *Latomus* 44: 33

Singleton, D. (1972) "Juvenal 6.120 and some ancient attitudes to the golden age," *G & R* 19: 151-64

----- (1983) "Juvenal's fifteenth Satire: a reading," *G & R* 30: 198-207

Smemo, E. (1937) "Zur Technik der Personenzeichnung bei Juvenal," *SO* 17: 77-102

Smith, W. S. Jr (1980) "Husband *vs.* wife in Juvenal's sixth Satire," *CW* 73: 323-32

Spaeth, J. W. (1942) "Persius on Epicurus: A note on Satires 3.83-84," *TAPA* 73: 119-22

Stahl, J. M. (1893) "Zu Juvenal Sat. VIII. 185-194," *RhM* 48: 157-60

Stanwell, H. B. (1888) "Persius, Sat. iii. 29," *CR* 2: 85

Stein, J. P. (1970) "The unity and scope of Juvenal's Fourteenth Satire," *CP* 65: 34-6

Streifinger, J. (1882) *Der Stil des Satirikers Juvenalis*, Regensburg

Stocker, C. W. (1845) *The Satires of Persius and Juvenal* (3rd edn.)

Strack, C. (1880) *De Juvenalis exilio*, Frankfurt

Sullivan, J. P. (ed.) (1963) *Critical Essays on Roman Literature 2: Satire*, Bloomington, London

----- (1968) *The Satyricon of Petronius: A Literary Study*, Bloomington, London

----- (1972) "In defence of Persius," *Ramus* 1: 48-62

Sweet, D. (1979) "Juvenal's Satire 4: poetic uses of indirection, *CSCA* 12: 283-303

Syme, R. (1979a) "The patria of Juvenal," *CP* 74: 1-15

----- (1979b) "Juvenal, Pliny, Tacitus," *AJP* 100: 250-78

----- (1982) "The marriage of Rubellius Blandus," *AJP* 103: 62-85

Tandoi, V. (1968) "Giovenale e il mecenatismo a Roma fra I e II secolo," *A & R* 13: 125-45

----- (1969) "Il recordo di Stazio 'dolce poeta' nella Sat. 7 di Giovenale," *Maia* 21: 103-22

Tartari, M. (1971) *"Brisaei venosus liber Acci* (Pers. 1.76)," *Maia* 23: 349-55

Tate, J. (1929) "Cornutus and the poets," *CQ* 23: 41-5

Tengström, E. (1980) *A Study of Juvenal's Tenth Satire*

Thiel, A. (1901) *Iuvenalis Graecissans* (Diss. Breslau)

Thomas, E. (1958) "Ovidian echoes in Juvenal," in *Ovidiana* 505-25

Townend, G. B. (1972) "The earliest scholiast on Juvenal," *CQ* 22: 376-87

----- (1973) "The literary substrata to Juvenal's Satires," *JRS* 63: 148-60

Ullman, B. L. (1950) "Psychological foreshadowing in the Satires of Horace and Juvenal," *AJP* 71: 408-16

----- (1960) "Epiraedia (Juvenal 8.66)," in *Hommages a L. Herrmann* 745-9

----- (1966) Miscellaneous comments on Juvenal," in *Studies in honour of H. Caplan* 274-84

Treloar, A. (1969) "Animae ebullitio," *Glotta* 47: 264-5

Vahlen, J. (1907) "Quaestiones Iuvenalianae," *Opuscula Academica* 1: 223-53

Vessey, D. W. T. C. (1973) "The Stoics and nobility: a philosophical theme," *Latomus* 32: 332-44

Vianello, N. (1935) *Giovenale: Satirae*, Turin

Vico, P. de (1961) *Pensiero Morale e religioso di Giovenale*, Naples

Villeneuve, F. (1918) *Essai sur Perse*, Paris

Vioni, G. (1972-3) "Considerazioni sulla settima satira di Giovenale," *RAIB* 61: 240-71

Wageningen, J. (1917) "Seneca et Iuvenalis," *Mnemosyne* 45: 417-29

Waszink, J. H. (1963) "Das Einleitungsgedicht des Persius," *WS* 76: 79-91

Waters, K. H. (1970) "Juvenal and the reign of Trajan," *Antichthon* 4: 62-77

Watson, G. R. (1952) "THETA NIGRUM," *JRS* 42: 56ff.

Watts, W. J. (1972) "A literary reminiscence in Juvenal (IX. 96)," *Latomus* 31: 519-20

Weidner, A. (1889) *D. Iunii Iuvenalis Saturae* (2nd edn.), Leipzig

Weinreich, O. (1949) *Römische Satiren*, Zürich

Weisinger, K. (1972) "Irony and Moderation in Juvenal 11, *CSCA* 5: 227-40

Wessner, P. (1931) *Scholia In Ivvenalem Vetvstiora*, Leipzig

West, M. L. (1961) "Persius i. 1-3," *CR* 11: 204

Weston, A. H. (1915) *Latin Satirical Writing Subsequent to Juvenal*, Diss. Yale Univ.

Widal, A. (1870) *Juvénal et ses Satires Etudes littéraires et morales* (2nd edn), Paris

Wiesen, D. S. (1963) "Juvenal's Moral Character: an Introduction," *Latomus* 22: 440-71

----- (1971) "Classis numerosa. Juvenal, Satire 7.151," *CQ* 21: 506-8

----- (1973) "Juvenal and the intellectuals," *Hermes* 101: 464-83

----- (1981) "A 'decency corruption' in Juvenal," *Eranos* 79: 99-103

Wilson, H. L. (1900) "The use of the simple for the compound verb in Juvenal," *TAPA* 31: 202-22

----- (1903) *D. Iunii Iuvenalis saturarum libri V*, Boston

Winkler, M. M. (1983) *The Persona in Three Satires of Juvenal*, Hildesheim, Zürich, New York

Witke, E. C. (1962a) "Juvenal 3, an eclogue for the urban poor," *Hermes* 90: 244-6

----- (1962b) "The Function of Persius' Choliambics," *Mnemosyne* 15: 151-8

----- (1970) *Latin satire: The Structure of Persuasion*, Leiden

Woodman, A. J. (1983) "Juvenal and Horace," *G & R* 30: 81-4

Yans, M. (1940) "Note sur l'établissement d'un passage de Juvénal," *AC* 57-64

Zetzel, J. E. G. (1977) "Lucilius, Lucretius, and Persius 1.1," *CP* 72: 40-2

Zicari, M. (1954) "A proposito di una accezione di venter," *RIL* 87: 188-92